General editor: Graham Ha

Brodie's

Hard Times

I. L. Baker

MACMILLAN

First published 1970 by James Brodie Ltd
Revised edition published 1976
by Pan Books Ltd

This revised edition published 1993 by
MACMILLAN PRESS LTD
Houndmills, Basingstoke, Hampshire RG21 6XS
and London
Companies and representatives
throughout the world

ISBN 0–333–58073–7

11 10 9 8 7 6 5 4 3 2
04 03 02 01 00 99 98 97 96 95

Printed in Great Britain by
Cox and Wyman Ltd
Reading, Berkshire

Contents

Preface by the general editor 5

To the student 6

The author and his work 8

Plot summary 12
Origin and purpose of the book 13
Background and setting 16

Chapter summaries, critical commentary, textual notes and revision questions 20

The characters 62
Mr Gradgrind 64
Mr Bounderby 66
Louisa Gradgrind 68
Thomas Gradgrind 69
Cecilia (Sissy) Jupe 71
Bitzer 73
Stephen Blackpool 74
Mrs Sparsit 75
Minor characters 77

Structure 79

Style 84

General questions and sample answer in note form 91

Preface

The intention throughout this study aid is to stimulate and guide, to encourage your involvement in the book, and to develop informed responses and a sure understanding of the main details.

Brodie's Notes provide a clear outline of the play or novel's plot, followed by act, scene, or chapter summaries and/or commentaries. These are designed to emphasize the most important literary and factual details. Poems, stories or non-fiction texts combine brief summary with critical commentary on individual aspects or common features of the genre being examined. Textual notes define what is difficult or obscure and emphasize literary qualities. Revision questions are set at appropriate points to test your ability to appreciate the prescribed book and to write accurately and relevantly about it.

In addition, each of these Notes includes a critical appreciation of the author's art. This covers such major elements as characterization, style, structure, setting and themes. Poems are examined technically – rhyme, rhythm, for instance. In fact, any important aspect of the prescribed work will be evaluated. The aim is to send you back to the text you are studying.

Each study aid concludes with a series of general questions which require a detailed knowledge of the book: some of these questions may invite comparison with other books, some will be suitable for coursework exercises, and some could be adapted to work you are doing on another book or books. Each study aid has been adapted to meet the needs of the current examination requirements. They provide a basic, individual and imaginative response to the work being studied, and it is hoped that they will stimulate you to acquire disciplined reading habits and critical fluency.

Graham Handley 1990

To the student

1 Reference in these Notes is by Book and Chapter (e.g. II, iii indicates Chapter Three of Book Two); any edition of the text may thus be used.

2 It is of the greatest importance for students to remember that they will be examined on the text itself, which must be read before using these Notes; they are in no way designed as a substitute for but as a supplement to a close reading of Dickens's work.

3 Background reading

The literature surrounding Dickens, the man and his work, is enormous; some guidance in general background reading may therefore be acceptable. However, students should not attempt to read through all the following: the relevant sections, guided by the index, will prove sufficient.

(a) **Biographies**

Charles Dickens: His Tragedy and Triumph, Edgar Johnson (Gollancz, 1953; revised and abridged Penguin, 1986).

The Making of Charles Dickens, Christopher Hibbert (Longmans Green, 1967; Penguin, 1983).

Dickens: A Life, Norman and Jeanne Mackenzie (OUP, 1979).

Dickens: A Biography, Fred Kaplan (Hodder & Stoughton, 1988).

Dickens, Peter Ackroyd (Sinclair-Stevenson, 1990; Minerva Paperback, 1991).

(b) **General**

Charles Dickens and Early Victorian England, R. J. Cruickshank (Pitman, 1949) is a useful, chatty and informative work of background history, manners, customs and social conditions.

In the *Pelican Guide to English Literature*, vol. VI: *From Dickens to Hardy*, edited by Boris Ford (Pelican, 1958) there is a stimulating essay on Dickens by R. C. Churchill.

(c) **Advanced students**

In *The Great Tradition* by the distinguished critic F. R. Leavis (Chatto & Windus, 1955) there is an appended note on *Hard Times* which attempts a revaluation of the novel in the light of its economic style and its serious subject-matter. This essay is a useful counterweight to the often expressed lack of appreciation of the novel by some literary critics.

Serious students should also look at George Orwell's essay *Charles Dickens*, in *Critical Essays* (Secker & Warburg, 1946) and other collections of critical material. This piece is quite indispensable, and is probably the best short article ever written on Dickens. Equally interesting are the following: Edmund Wilson's essay on Dickens in *The Wound and the Bow* (W. H. Allen, 1941), *Dickens at Work*, J. Butt and K. Tillotson (Methuen, 1957), and *Charles Dickens: A Critical Introduction*, K. J. Fielding (Longmans, 1958). Other useful material can be found in *Dickens: Modern Judgements*, A. E. Dyson (Macmillan, 1968) and in *Hard Times*, *Great Expectations*, and *Our Mutual Friend* edited by N. Page, in the *Macmillan Casebook Series* (1979). A sound critical appreciation is also to be found as a preface in recent updated editions of the novel in the Penguin series.

4 A great deal of valuable information is contained in *The Dickensian*, a magazine published regularly by the Dickens Fellowship; however, copies are generally available only in the largest reference libraries, the British Museum Reading Room and Library and, by appointment, at the Dickens House in London. The present author gratefully acknowledges the assistance of the late editor, Mr Leslie C. Staples and more recently, of Assistant Curator Jane Ramsay for their help in pursuing certain points in these Notes, and in particular for directing his attention to the issues of June and September 1952, in which T. W. Hill briefly annotated the text of the novel.

The author and his work

Charles John Huffham (or Huffam) Dickens (7 February 1812–9 June 1870) was born at Landport, Portsea, near Portsmouth, where his father, John Dickens, was a clerk in the Navy Pay Office. Both his parents were descended from old-established families which had come down in the world. Before long the family moved about between Chatham and London, and Dickens's father, a cheerful but ineffective and voluble individual, managed to get himself seriously in debt. His mother, in an attempt to avoid financial disaster, took a house in Gower Street as an 'Establishment' for the education of Anglo-Indian children: this was not a success. In 1824 the household possessions were sold up (the sensitive twelve-year-old Charles being considered the fittest person to negotiate with the pawnbroker), and the father – the prototype of the immortal Mr Micawber – was sent to the Marshalsea prison for debt, Mrs Dickens and the younger children accompanying him as was usual in those days: the situation will be familiar to readers of *Little Dorrit*. Charles was handed over to the care of an old lady in Camden Town, and went to work, a small sickly child, in a blacking-factory on a Thames-side wharf, at a wage of six shillings a week. He was, in his own words, 'miserably unhappy', and 'I know that, but for the mercy of God, I might easily have been, for any care that was taken of me, a little robber or a little vagabond'. The misery and indignity of this life and the hardships and mortifications suffered by a delicate and sensitive child (the basis of the early chapters of *David Copperfield*) affected him so deeply that when he grew up he could never bear to speak of them, although all his books contain some element, scene or recollection from these depressing days.

After three months' imprisonment a fortunate and opportune legacy enabled Mr Dickens to pay his debts and obtain his release: soon afterwards he retired from his official duties on a pension, and Charles was able to return to school and continue on more regular lines his love of reading, especially of the older novelists, such as Fielding, Smollett and Goldsmith. The kindness of relations enabled him to visit the theatre, the love of which remained with him for the rest of his life, and to which he was drawn for a time as a career. At the age of fifteen he became a junior clerk in a lawyer's office, occupying his leisure time with extensive reading, particularly at the British Museum, and learning shorthand, at which he became very expert. Soon he was reporting in the Law Courts; finding the work tedious, he decided to become a parliamentary reporter for the *True Sun*, and later the *Mirror of Parliament* and the *Morning Chronicle*. He enjoyed particularly travelling to political meetings all over the country and meeting all sorts of people. He contributed his first published sketch (December, 1833) to the *Monthly Magazine*, and then other pieces followed in the *Evening Chronicle* (1835), in which, a year later, appeared the collection *Sketches by Boz*, a pseudonym adopted from the nickname of a young brother.

The years 1836–7 proved the turning-point of his life. In 1836 he married Catherine Hogarth, daughter of George Hogarth, the manager of the *Morning Chronicle*. In March 1836 the first number of *The Posthumous Papers of the Pickwick Club* appeared, and after the arrival of Sam Weller in the fifth number, the new serial took the country by storm. Dickens had become a famous author: his struggling days were over. In 1836 too he accepted the editorship of the monthly magazine *Bentley's Miscellany*, in which *Oliver Twist* was serialised. Thenceforward Dickens's literary career was a continued success, with overlapping serials following one another with remarkable rapidity: *Nicholas Nickleby* in 1838–9, and later *The Old Curiosity Shop* and *Barnaby Rudge* (Dickens's only historical novel, except for part of *A Tale of Two Cities*). In addition to all this he burdened himself for twenty years with the editorship of his own weekly magazine *Household Words*, and later

All the Year Round. In 1841 he went to America, where he was enthusiastically welcomed, a reception somewhat dampened, however, by the publication of the highly critical *American Notes* and *Martin Chuzzlewit*; then came the *Christmas Books* of *A Christmas Carol* and *The Chimes*. In 1844 Dickens went to Italy, to Genoa, where he completed *The Chimes*; he then wrote *The Cricket on the Hearth* and two lesser-known stories *The Battle of Life* and *The Haunted Man*. In 1846 he visited Switzerland, and while there he wrote *Dombey and Son* (published 1848); *David Copperfield* followed (1849–50), then *Bleak House* (1852–3), *Hard Times* in 1854, and *Little Dorrit* in 1856–7.

Dickens was at the peak of his fame: but domestic troubles clouded his success. Incompatibility of temper with his wife reached an irrevocable pitch in 1858, in which year they separated (Catherine having borne him ten children), and for the rest of his life his sister-in-law, Georgiana Hogarth, kept house for him. He had by then removed to Gadshill Place, near Rochester, Kent, where he lived until his death.

In 1858 he began his public readings from his works, financially rewarding indeed, but such was the strain that they seriously impaired his constitution and undoubtedly hastened his death. In 1859 *Household Words* was incorporated in a new journal, *All the Year Round*, in which appeared *A Tale of Two Cities* (1859), *The Uncommercial Traveller* (1860), and *Great Expectations* (1860–61). *Our Mutual Friend* came next in 1864–5. All this time Dickens was continuing his public readings, and travelling about endlessly within the country and abroad. In 1865 he was involved in a terrible railway accident, at Staplehurst, in Kent, in which, although himself physically uninjured (he helped to extricate the dead and succour the dying) he sustained severe nervous shock. Nevertheless, at the end of 1867 he went again to America, where he enjoyed a magnificent reception and £20,000 profits: but he had to abandon much of his tour on medical advice. He was broken in nerves, and a martyr to insomnia. In 1869 he started his

last work, *The Mystery of Edwin Drood*, interrupted and un-
finished by his death from an apoplectic seizure. He died at
the height of his powers at only 58 and he lies buried in the
Poets' Corner of Westminster Abbey, the last resting-place of
many celebrated British men of letters and the arts.

Plot summary

Hard Times was the ninth, and of the greater novels, the shortest work of Dickens. The plot, for one of his novels, is remarkably uncomplicated, and moves forward directly and chronologically.

Thomas Gradgrind, a retired hardware wholesaler, professes to rule his life and those dependent on him according to fact, logic, calculation: the fundamental creed of Utilitarianism. His friend, Josiah Bounderby, is a millowner and banker, who professes to have lifted himself from the gutter by inflexible adherence to the same principles. A young girl, Cecilia (Sissy) Jupe is abandoned by her circus-clown father in Coketown and is taken to the home of the Gradgrinds. Gradgrind's son Thomas is a selfish and rather cunning rascal, who is to go into Bounderby's bank when he is old enough. Louisa, his sister, eventually marries Bounderby, but without affection, and is used by Tom both before and after her marriage to further his own ends. Even this, however, is not sufficient to cover his needs, especially those of his gambling debts, and he takes money from the bank, so arranging matters that it appears that a robbery has been committed. Suspicion is immediately directed upon Stephen Blackpool, an honest workman who has fallen foul of his workmates and their Union leader, and of Bounderby's stubbornness and temper, and who, after having been 'sent to Coventry', leaves Bounderby's mill. Louisa, meanwhile, innocent of worldly matters through her upbringing, plans to elope with James Harthouse, a languid political agent who has attached himself to the 'Hard Fact' school in Coketown. The arrangements for the elopement are overheard by the prying Mrs Sparsit, Bounderby's housekeeper of lady-like pretensions: she seizes the opportunity of doing some mischief to Louisa by hurrying the news to her employer. Bounderby, in turn, rushes off to tell Gradgrind, but finds not only that his wife has forestalled him, but is actually sheltering in her father's house. Bounderby refuses to listen to Gradgrind's protestations and notions that, perhaps after all, their system has its defects, and he renounces Louisa, who remains with her father in his household, now, after Mrs Gradgrind's pathetic death, much more genial under Sissy Jupe's influence.

A reward is offered for the arrest of Stephen Blackpool, who has left Coketown and changed his name in order to secure work. His friend Rachael, who knows all about his domestic troubles with a debauched and drunken wife, endeavours to clear his name, and ultimately she and Sissy come upon him mortally injured at the bottom of a disused pit-shaft, into which he had fallen while making his way back with his true version of his activities. Enough is said before he dies to incriminate Tom, who, by Sissy's aid, steals away from Coketown. His father follows him, as does Bitzer, a protégé of Bounderby, and the selfish sulky product of 'the system' is saved from complete ignominy only by the help of Sissy's old friends of the circus, led by Sleary. Gradgrind is able to effect his son's escape: but he publicly exonerates Blackpool and accuses his son. Bounderby dies in a fit; Louisa is to find some happiness at the last with Sissy's children, and Gradgrind himself, despite criticism, sorts out afresh his ideas, now knowing the futility of eliminating love and kindness from human life and relationships.

Origin and purpose of the book

Dickens completed *Bleak House* at the end of August 1853 in his magazine *Household Words*, which by then had been running for some eighteen months, but the financial position of the periodical was poor and circulation was shrinking. Dickens's friends and partners suggested that he should remedy this unhappy state of affairs by writing a new serial in weekly numbers: 'There is such a fixed idea on the part of my printers and co-partners in *Household Words*, that a story of me, continued from week to week, would make some unheard of effect with it that I am going to write one.' This he wrote to Miss Coutts, a family friend, on 23 January 1854; but he had already turned the idea over in his mind to such an extent that he had sent his friend Forster, three days earlier, a list of fourteen titles asking him to look at them. They were: According to Cocker, Prove it, Stubborn Things, Mr Gradgrind's Facts, The Grindstone, Hard Times, Two and Two are Four, Something Tangible, Our Hardheaded Friend, Rust and Dust, Simple Arithmetic, A Matter of Calculation, A Mere Question of Figures, The Gradgrind Philosophy; other titles in the manuscript were: Fact, Hard-headed Gradgrind, Hard Heads and Soft Hearts, Heads and Tales, and Black and White. From these it is already apparent that Dickens had decided on the nature and scope of his story long before he started the actual planning and writing.

And there were other sources apart from the necessity of rescuing the shrinking circulation of his magazine. All Dickens's novels contain something of his personal and deeply-felt emotions, and something of his antagonism to the wrongs and evils of society. He rarely suggests solutions: but he does convey the inhumanity of man to man, and is always urging for a renewal of the real Christian spirit in human relationships. In the first number of *Household Words* (30 March 1850) he had declared that its policy would be to keep a sharp look-out for what was wrong, that it would fight for tolerance and the progress of human welfare, and would give no quarter to exposed chicanery and oppression. A part of this address is worth quoting in full, bearing in mind the message of *Hard Times* itself, not to appear for four years:

... No mere utilitarian spirit, no iron binding of the mind to grim realities, will give a harsh tone to our *Household Words*. In the bosoms of the young and old, of the well-to-do and of the poor, we would tenderly cherish that light of Fancy which is inherent in the human breast; which, according to its nurture, burns with an inspiring flame, or sinks into a sullen glare, but which (or woe betide that day!) can never be extinguished.

The goal of society was a loving union of the masses of human lives in generous feeling and noble purpose, not harsh business efficiency or the grinding of an economic machine. Subsequent numbers dealt specifically, and strongly, with sanitary reform, social and municipal progress, law and crime, and, of course, with much lighter and more general matters, but the workings of society, its outstanding evils and contrasts, distressed Dickens constantly, and he exposed a great deal of it in *Bleak House*. Though exhausted from this enormous work, the idea for his next, as he said, '... laid hold of me by the throat in a very violent manner'. Others, particularly Carlyle, had discussed, often vehemently and violently, the 'Condition of England': Dickens knew Carlyle's work well and, indeed, dedicated *Hard Times* to him. In his widespread travels about the country he had noticed much, and it is thus difficult to say which particular town Coketown is supposed to represent, or which particular industry is being discussed. Certainly it is difficult to grasp what exactly goes on in Bounderby's mill. Further details on these points will be examined in the section on Background, but the general purpose is quite clear: a further exposure of society, this time in an industrial setting, emphasising the evils and constrictions of a mechanical utilitarian system in which love and affection play no part.

It should be added here that Dickens prepared the ground with his usual thoroughness, studying the Education Board's questions for their examinations of teachers, visiting Preston (see section on Background), and struggling all the time with his first weekly serial since *Master Humphrey's Clock* (1840–41) and the special problem of brevity necessary for his magazine. As he wrote, 'The difficulty of the space is CRUSHING. Nobody can have an idea of it who has not had an experience of patient fiction-writing with some elbow-room always, and open places in perspective. In this form, with any kind of regard to the current number, there is absolutely no such thing.' Dickens had to learn a new discipline, excluding material and economising in detail (see Style), for within each weekly number of about eight pages of script he had to present his characters, sketch in background and create the appropriate atmosphere. Endlessly planning, sometimes groaning aloud in his correspondence [e.g. 'I am in a dreary state, planning and planning the story of *Hard Times* (out of materials for I don't know how long a story)'], he was eventually forced to expand his weekly instalments to ten pages of his manuscript. Dickens pressed on. The first number appeared in *Household Words* on 1 April 1854. The story doubled the circulation within the first ten weeks. He wrote on, often tired and dreary with the work, taking a holiday in France in June and early July but still writing away furiously: his correspondents received such agonised cries as, 'Bobbing up, corkwise from a sea of Hard Times', and 'stunned with work'. To Forster he wrote, 'I am three parts mad, and the fourth delirious, with perpetual rushing at Hard Times, I have done what I hope is a good thing with Stephen, taking his story as a whole ... I have been looking forward through so many weeks and sides of paper to this Stephen business that now – as usual – it being over, I feel as if nothing in the world, in the way of intense and violent rushing hither and thither, could quite restore my balance.' He wrote the last lines in a wild burst of energy two days before he had expected, and felt appallingly 'used up', no great surprise after having written 120,000 words in just over five months.

Background and setting

The physical setting of *Hard Times*, limited to Coketown, is simply explained: it could be anywhere in the industrial Midlands or north of England. Various attempts have been made to locate the aptly-named fictitious town, which is no doubt a composite picture made up of Dickens's recollections of various places such as Preston (see below), Manchester,

Wolverhampton and Birmingham: we do in fact know that Dickens had already chosen the title and written several chapters before his visit to Preston itself. It is generally considered that he went there, however, to gain some 'local colour' for his story, as there had been a strike among its cotton-mill workers which had lasted twenty-three weeks, one of a succession in the Lancashire towns. Dickens did not much favour Preston: it was quiet and orderly despite the stubbornness of the strike, and he wrote to Forster that 'I am afraid I shall not be able to get much here'. He may have intended to introduce a strike into *Hard Times*: but he told Mrs Gaskell, who was currently working on another industrial novel, that, 'I have no intention of striking. The monstrous claims at domination made by a certain class of manufacturers, and the extent to which the way is made easy for working men to slide down into discontent under such hands, are within my scheme; but I am not going to strike.'

Here we come upon the difficulty of separating the purpose and background of *Hard Times*: it is in fact impossible. In this compact, bitter novel the background is the purpose: this revelation of people's attitudes in an industrial and utilitarian atmosphere is Dickens's intention, although, as will be seen, it is even more than this finally and eventually.

Social analysis in various forms had been a theme of Dickens from his earliest works: to take random examples, one may note the attitudes towards stealing, murder, employment and welfare of children in *Oliver Twist*; even the prison scenes of *Pickwick Papers* are illuminating and provoking. With *Dombey and Son* we watch the sordid workings of a monetary society, emphasised (more humorously, certainly) in *A Christmas Carol*. *David Copperfield* abounds in social comment, especially when it concerns itself with Doctors' Commons, child labour and the money-mindedness of Spenlow and Uriah Heep. *Bleak House*, immediately preceding *Hard Times*, gained in ruthlessness of exposition: the whole rotten workings of the social system are there detailed and commented upon, save for one feature – the industrial or mechanised side of life under the power of single-minded, bigoted, self-made men. This aspect of acquisitive society is the theme, background and purpose of *Hard Times*, which thus forms part of Dickens's own developing notions and sympathies.

It is in fact important to see *Hard Times* in its proper perspective. There is no space here to detail the several evils of Victorian society: the books recommended and any good text-book of economic history will provide, if needed, the factual background. *Hard Times* comments harshly on certain key characteristics of that society, in particular its rule and conduct of affairs without sympathy and love, which, in Dickens's opinion, destroys all the moral virtues. With an educational system which condemns fancy and the love of life (Book I, i–ii), with self-interest as the springboard of personal and governmental action, all men, in all relationships, will be led into conflict and bitterness. In the tightly-woven plot of *Hard Times* we see this played out to the logical end. Thus the book is not merely a study of industrial capitalism, born by the Preston strike. Dickens had been thinking over and developing a wider, broader theme for years. In fact the Preston affair was a minor influence, and as it stood even a misleading one. There was in fact no Trades Union among the spinners and weavers of that date; the men's leaders (compare Slackbridge, Book II, iv and Book III, iv) were not permanent organisers, but local workmen. It is not merely as a study of industrial organisation or capitalism that *Hard Times* draws its strength and purpose, but as a moral fable. It attacks society, certainly, but not as Shaw and Chesterton suggest, on the side of labour and to arouse other bitternesses: it is certainly not on the side of capitalism either. It is based on Christian morality (or the whole story of Stephen Blackpool's life, struggles and death is pointless and even ludicrous): on Dickens's sincere belief that society should be invested with greater humility and charity, and should return to a simple Christian faith of doing good to others (see particularly in this connection Book I, ix; and the many Biblical allusions). Its coherence and power lie in this unity of purpose and background, and make it topical not merely for Dickens's own day and time, but for all time when the workings of society lead to enormous distinctions of wealth and happiness, of misery and success.

Two terms remain to be explained: utilitarianism and *laissez-faire*. The first is the name given to a system of ethics which sets up as the rule of conduct the best interests either of the individual or of the community. The system was given a scientific basis by Jeremy Bentham (1748–1832), whose object was the greatest happiness of the greatest number (taking no account of the quality of pleasure), and extended by J. S. Mill (1806–73), who included happiness in his statement of the doctrine. Incidentally, it may be noted that J. S. Mill in his childhood (taught principally by his father, another philosopher, historian and economist) underwent the most rigorous schooling, learning by the age of fourteen an enormous range of subjects, including political economy, history, mathematics, classical literature and logic. It may be said in general that Dickens was influenced by Benthamism, and shared many of the aims of radical reform of the Utilitarians, but he always refused to accept the 'colder' wing of the sect, who preferred abstract theory rather than the actual welfare of human beings. The term 'laissez-faire' (French for 'let it alone') is a political and economic term, referring to those who advocated unrestricted competition, or the minimum of interference with industry. The whole of *Hard Times* is a withering attack on this belief.

Chapter summaries, critical commentary, textual notes and revision questions

Book the first. Sowing

Chapter I
The One Thing Needful. In a school-room a hard grim dry-looking man is emphasising to the children the prime need of teaching and learning nothing but facts.

Dickens's chapter headings were always as carefully considered and preplanned as was the rest of his thinking about the tone, intention and structure of his work. The reference to and implication of 'The One Thing Needful' would not have been missed by most of his Victorian readers, who were well acquainted with the Scriptures. This graphic, unyielding opening monologue sets the scene, the tone and the motivation – heavy with irony, metaphor and savage humour – of the entire novel. Both the initial short speech and the subsequent physical description of the yet-unnamed speaker are studded with deliberate repetition: stressing, emphasising the stubbornness of dogma in mind, body and spirit, especially when directed with such aggressive force towards the impressionable minds of children as a captive and cowed audience. The adult world, oppressive, commanding, grasping and acquisitive, is set against the innocence, gullibility and weakness of the child: the 'One thing needful', but missing, should be a blend of tolerance, patience, understanding, open-mindedness and imaginative freedom, not submission to 'Fact' and dogma. Dickens has expressed, albeit ironically and in parody, a principle of moral, social and religious duty – a 'philosophy of life' as it should be practised: this is a persistent feature of his many and varied works.

The One Thing Needful This is a reference to the Gospel story (Luke, x. 42) of the two sisters Martha and Mary on the occasion of a visit by Jesus to their home. Martha the elder sister was the anxious, bustling preoccupied housekeeper, while her sister sat and listened quietly, profiting by the presence and wisdom of their honoured guest. When Martha complained that Mary was idle, Jesus mildly rebuked the elder sister, saying that Mary had chosen 'the one thing needful'.

commodious cellarage Ample room (the metaphor implies cavernous depths).

inclined plane of little vessels i.e. the sloping school-room floor, with the desks and their little occupants.

Chapter II
Murdering the Innocents. The speaker is Thomas Gradgrind, a firm believer in the supremacy of facts and figures in all departments of life. The children are questioned by him, the schoolmaster, Mr M'Choakumchild, and a Government Schools Inspector, eliciting imaginative – and therefore un-acceptable – replies from Cecilia (Sissy) Jupe, the daughter of a circus performer, and correct factual dry-as-dust responses from a colourless fair-complexioned boy named Bitzer.

Again, the chapter title, ironically, has a biblical associa-tion, and forms part of Dickens's indictment of factual learn-ing by rote, opening up the scene to name three of the principal characters (out of 26) of the entire novel: Thomas Gradgrind, Sissy (Cecilia) Jupe, and Bitzer (forename never given). Each, together with the School Inspector and the sardonically-named new teacher Mr M'Choakumchild, helps to develop the theme of Fact versus Fancy (that is, imagina-tion). The two children are vividly contrasted: the boy cold, wan, fact-bound; the girl is timid, polite, imaginative. The last two paragraphs are a triumph of Dickens's blend of bitter humour and controlled anger, hurled at the principles and practice of formal education.

Murdering the Innocents Biblically, Herod's massacre of the children of Bethlehem under two years old, with the design of destroying the infant Jesus (see Matthew, ii. 16).

galvanising apparatus Galvanism is electricity developed by chemical action: here the essential meaning is stimulating, as with a powerful current.

Girl number twenty There were so many pupils in the large classes of Dickens's time that they were given numbers for easy reference and identification.

breaks Tames.

graminivorous Grass-eating.

incisive Properly (of teeth) incisor, a cutting or fore-tooth.

bolus A large pill.

fistic phraseology Expressions connected with boxing.

cosmography A description of the world. We should now call this geography.

Her Majesty's most Honourable Privy Council's Schedule B At this date (1854) there was no Board or Ministry of Education. Such government interest that existed was organised through the Committee of Council (Privy Council) on Education. Schedule B, instituted in 1846, detailed the Syllabus of Qualifications of Pupil Teachers during each year of training, and included all the subjects listed by Dickens in the text.

compound proportion An arithmetical term for a type of calculation involving ratios.

Morgiana in the Forty Thieves An apt allusion, for Morgiana was Ali Baba's servant in the story of *Ali Baba and the Forty Thieves*: she killed off a gang of thieves who were plotting against her master by pouring boiling oil into the leather oil-jars in which they had concealed themselves.

Chapter III

A Loophole. Returning home from the school in a flush of self-satisfaction, Mr Gradgrind reflects on his own five model children, all nurtured from infancy in an atmosphere of hard fact. Approaching his symmetrical and practical home, Stone Lodge, on the outskirts of the town, he hears the noise of the travelling fair and horse-riding show, run by Sleary and his troupe. He sees children peeping through the back, and recognises among them, with considerable amazement, two of his own children. Louisa seems self-willed (despite her bringing-up) and defiant; Tom seems a weaker child. They are led home in disgrace, Mr Gradgrind reflecting all the while on what Mr Bounderby would say about this delinquency.

This develops the Fact versus Fancy theme, skilfully introducing the Jupe circus presence and two of Gradgrind's five children. Already these are shown to differ in character and personality, the girl defiant, the boy abased and speechless, apparently furtive and subservient. Significantly there are the slightest hints of Gradgrind's affection for his children, of Louisa's vague, struggling consciousness that there must be something more to life than a regimen of facts and practicality, and of some apprehension concerning a Mr Bounderby. Already, therefore, there has been established a subtle inter-linking of the three households: the Gradgrinds, the Jupes, and Bounderby. Dickens had now given subscribers to his periodical *Household Words* their first instalment (three chapters) of his novel, a good solid read on Saturday 1 April 1854, to be continued without interruption every Saturday until 12 August of the same year.

Great Bear Ursa Major, one of the constellations. See note on 'Charles's Wain', below.

Professor Owen Sir Richard Owen (1804–1892), a professor of Comparative Anatomy and a prolific writer and research worker in anatomical and fossil studies.

Charles's Wain The seven bright stars in Ursa Major, also called the Plough.

cow with the crumpled horn One of the animals in the ancient but ever-popular nursery rhyme of *The House that Jack Built*.

Tom Thumb Title of a fairy story by Charles Perrault (1628–1703), who also wrote *Puss in Boots*, *Cinderella* and *The Sleeping Beauty*.

Coketown Any northern industrial town fits the picture, and we know that Dickens went to Preston for some 'local colour'.

conchological Concerned with the study or science of shells.

Peter Piper The popular alliterative nursery rhyme; it usually reads,

> Peter Piper picked a peck of pickled pepper;
> A peck of pickled pepper Peter Piper picked;
> If Peter Piper picked a peck of pickled pepper
> Where's the peck of pickled pepper Peter Piper picked?

suffrages Votes (here, of confidence).

Tyrolean Of the Tyrol, at this date a province of Austria–Hungary, now the most westerly province of Austria.

Merrylegs Aptly named: one of the few dogs (six in all) named in Dickens's works. Dickens himself enjoyed the company of many dogs throughout his life, including a spaniel, a bloodhound and a St Bernard.

Mr William Button A hippo-comedietta is a circus show in which most of the 'characters' act on horseback (see III. vii): apparently the play named was one of these. Billy Button was the pet name for any small boy donning his first pair of breeches. Dickens was very fond of Amateur and Benefit theatricals, writing many short plays himself, and knew a great deal about the theatre. (See 'The Author and his Work', p. 8).

Mrs Grundy The question 'What will Mrs Grundy say?' is from Thomas Morton's play *Speed the Plough* (1798): Mrs Grundy epitomises conventional prudery.

Chapter IV
Mr Bounderby. At Stone Lodge Mr Bounderby is haranguing Mrs Gradgrind, a colourless ineffective woman, about his favourite topic – himself. He is a middle-aged, self-centred, boastful and pompous man, who prides himself, martyr-like, on his being self-made, his mother having abandoned him to a harsh grandmother. Mr Gradgrind appears with his two crestfallen children, who are soon dismissed to their studies: the men decide that their disobedience must have been caused by the influence of Cecilia (Sissy) Jupe, whom they decide to dismiss from the school.

A further neat linking chapter finds Mr Bounderby and Mrs Gradgrind in conversation at Stone Lodge, the one large, boastful, monopolising and rude, the lady feeble, meek and spiritless. The detail of Bounderby's birth and upbringing is as monotonous as it is – to us – amusing, obviously well-rehearsed and practised. The speech rhythms (read some of it aloud) reflect its exaggeration and pomposity, just as the few remarks of Mrs Gradgrind reveal her mental and physical weakness and subservience to the principles of the school of Fact. There are insights here into the stifling atmosphere of Stone Lodge and all it stands for, the consequent surging rebelliousness and misery of fact-afflicted children, and how Bounderby, Louisa and Cecilia Jupe are being individualised and firmly integrated into the fabric of the story.

St Giles's Church St Giles's, Cripplegate, an old London church founded in 1090.

kettle of fish Properly, a disagreeable or awkward state of things; here, one of Bounderby's preposterous expressions.

a question of figures That is, she had money of her own!

strollers Itinerant actors.

'Turn ... to the right about' The noun phrase 'to the right about', usually military in the sense of a complete change of march-direction, here means to send packing, to dismiss or turn away unceremoniously.

Adam Smith British economist (1723–1790), whose most important work was *The Wealth of Nations* (1776) which had a great influence on political and economic thought. Some of its theories have been discarded since, however.

Malthus Thomas Robert Malthus (1766–1834), a British economist, whose theory of population (1798) was fiercely criticised; he maintained that the natural tendency of population was to increase faster than the means of subsistence, and that it was therefore controlled by want and all its attendant miseries.

pipeclay A fine white kind of clay which forms a paste with water and was, as its name suggests, used to make clay pipes.

Revision questions on Chapters I–IV

1 Describe the appearance of Thomas Gradgrind Senior, his wife and Mr Bounderby.

2 What information has so far been revealed about the early life of Mr Bounderby?

3 How many children comprise the Gradgrind family? Name them, and describe their home and activities.

4 How would you describe the attitude of Mr Gradgrind to his children, and of Louisa to her father and to Mr Bounderby?

5 Think of one or two appropriate adjectives applicable to Bitzer, Thomas and Mr Bounderby.

Chapter V
The Key-note. Here Coketown is described: a smoke-blackened industrial town, a matter-of-fact and monotonous

town, whose people knew little relaxation and pleasure apart from that which has to be taken furtively or illegally. During their walk Mr Gradgrind and Mr Bounderby encounter Cecilia Jupe, who is being chased by Bitzer, who as usual, parades his 'factual' servility: the girl, out to obtain a liniment for her father's circus bruises, leads the town-magnates to her home above a public-house, telling them not to fear Merrylegs, Jupe's dog.

Here the appropriately-named Coketown, the physical background to the novel, is vividly described. Its restricting monotony and dull uniformity, the all-pervading noise, pollution, its over-all soul-destroying drabness of itself and the lives of its inhabitants, mirror the bleakness of its economic and political base: the philosophy of the Gradgrind–Bounderby school of thought. The main characters so far described are now further linked, and there is another faint suggestion that Gradgrind may have (not yet quite consciously, perhaps) a latent streak of kindness embedded somewhere in his nature.

head of an elephant An apt description of the huge pivoted beam which relayed the power of early steam machinery from the piston to the crank-shaft, and was forever, inexorably and monotonously, plunging up and down.
lying-in hospital Maternity hospital.
Mocha coffee A fine coffee, first brought from Mocha, on the Red Sea.
There was an old woman A very old nursery rhyme indeed.
nine oils This is clearly some form of liniment. One medical authority has located its formula in a nineteenth-century household pharmacopoeia, and it must be remembered that nine is a magical number with attendant effects.

Chapter VI
Sleary's Horsemanship. Sissy is unable to find her father, and much surprised, goes off to look for him elsewhere. The waiting men are confronted by another of the circus acts, a Mr E. W. B. Childers and his diminutive assistant Kidderminster. These tell the Coketown worthies that Jupe, getting too old for

the circus-life, has been failing of late, and that he has abandoned his daughter so that she should not be hurt and embarrassed by his decline: she is to improve her education. Sleary's company, the various acts of the show-ground, assemble in the room: Sleary himself enters, and then the bewildered Sissy Jupe returns, and realises her position. Mr Gradgrind proposes to take care of Sissy, so long as she cuts off her connection with the show-people. Arrangements are concluded, and Sissy goes away with her new guardian.

In what is probably the longest chapter in Book the First (in fact, the only chapter of sixteen in Book I to provide by itself a weekly instalment of the serial) we move from Fact to Fancy in the Gradgrind–Bounderby encounter; first with E. W. B. Childers and his circus 'child' assistant, and then with the proprietor Mr Sleary and the rest of his troupe. The essence here is that of decision-making. Signor Jupe has decided to leave, Gradgrind and Bounderby will have to decide on the fate of the abandoned child and, above all, Sissy herself must, under severe restriction, arrive at a lasting and fateful decision. Sleary's speech defect (is this an obstacle to one's reading of the text?) and the obvious affection felt by him and his troupe for Sissy, render the scene (and indeed Gradgrind) sympathetic but not sentimental. The background is of colour, variety, tolerance, affection: there is rich entertainment and even poignancy in the development of the action, and a significant bond has been created between the Gradgrind family (the Fact element) and Sissy Jupe (the Fancy, the imaginative counterweight).

Pegasus's Arms In Greek mythology, Pegasus was the winged horse which sprang from Medusa's blood: later, it was associated with the Muses, and the name is used for the inspiration of poetry.

Good malt ... find it handy Such verses are common on inn-signs, and this particular example is known to have been written on the sign-board of the Malt Shovel Inn at the foot of Chatham Hill, Kent.

Newmarket coat A close-fitting coat, originally a riding-coat, named after the racing town.

Centaur In Greek mythology, a fabulous monster, half-man, half-horse.

white bismuth Bismuth is a grey-white metallic element: one of its combinations is called Pearl White, and is sometimes used as a pigment.

carmine A red pigment.

stow that Stop it (slang).

pay your ochre Pay your money (or gold); another slang expression.

goosed Hissed of the stage (slang).

Dick Jones of Wapping The phrase may be taken to mean a person of little or no importance. Wapping is (and was) a London district lying between the old London Docks area and the Pool of London. Dickens, an inveterate wanderer even at night, knew well what he called 'the darker side of London life'. In his day Wapping (and other areas of 'poverty, misery and vice') was hostile to outsiders. VIPs and other visitors were escorted by police inspectors.

by the Lord Harry One of the Devil's (more jocular) names was Lord Harry: Congreve (whose plays were well known to Dickens) uses this same oath.

ciphering Arithmetic.

one fixed eye Dickens was apparently fascinated by oddness in eyes. The curious might look up the descriptions of Newman Noggs in *Nicholas Nickleby*, Captain Bunsby in *Dombey and Son* and Mr Grummer in *Pickwick*.

morrithed Morrised, got away speedily, decamped, in Sleary's 'pursy' pronunciation (slang).

I'll pound it I'll wager a pound on it.

pursy Puckered.

Chapter VII

Mrs Sparsit. Mr Bounderby's housekeeper is Mrs Sparsit, a widow of considerable high-born and family pretensions, with a bedridden great-aunt Lady Scadgers. Mrs Sparsit and her employer discuss Mr Gradgrind's whim in taking over Sissy Jupe, who is at the moment at his (Bounderby's) house. Bounderby talks of his past hard life, comparing it with Mrs Sparsit's days in fashionable society. Mr Gradgrind calls, with his daughter Louisa, and takes Sissy off to Stone Lodge for her future training in 'the system'.

It is a measure of the eventual importance of this eccentric character that Dickens awards her a chapter to herself: there is obvious relish and humour in the author's ironic description of her ancestry, pretensions and aspirations. She is also the butt of Bounderby's preposterous bluster. However, the signs are clear that her humility is assumed and false and that she has designs (as a long-time widow) on her own and Bounderby's future.

relict Widow.

blind-hookey A card game of chance, in which one must stake money without looking at one's cards.

a mysterious leg A humorous turn of phrase implying that the old lady had long been bedridden with an undefined (and perhaps non-existent?) ailment.

Coriolanian Gaius Coriolanus was a legendary hero of ancient Rome: he represents (as readers of Shakespeare's play of the name will know) arrogant and unbending aristocracy. Here the term simply means 'Roman', and the 'typical' Roman nose was high-bridged.

Habeas Corpus The Latin for 'Thou shalt have the body'; a legal term, meaning a writ requiring the production in court of the body of a person who has been imprisoned, so that the lawfulness of the imprisonment may be investigated. The Habeas Corpus Act dates from 1679.

Bill of Rights A measure adopted by the Parliament of 1689 condemning the interference of the Crown with Civil Liberty: it restored the monarchy to its constitutional position.

'Prince and lords ... has made,' Two lines from Goldsmith's *Deserted Village*.

Italian Opera The name of the theatre which rose from the ashes of the burnt down King's Theatre in 1791: in 1837 the name was again changed, this time in honour of Queen Victoria's coronation, to Her Majesty's Theatre. The Arcade mentioned by Bounderby was the Royal Opera Arcade running at the back of the original building, linking Pall Mall and Charles Street, but his details seem (as usual) to be fabricated and lying, for this Arcade was closed and locked at each end every night.

link A torch made of tow and pitch, formerly used for lighting people along the streets.

Mayfair District of West London to the north of Piccadilly. It is covered by once fashionable streets and squares, where the aristocracy had their town houses. Its name remains as a symbol of high society.

Dwarf, and the Hunchback A tale of the *Arabian Nights Entertainments*. (See note, p. 29 on 'Sultan ... story'.) Dickens was very fond of his collection of ancient Oriental tales. In *David Copperfield*, in a literally autobiographical piece, he writes: 'They (various early novels) kept alive my fancy ... they, and the *Arabian Nights*, and the *Tales of the Genii* – and did me no harm; for, whatever harm was in some of them, was not there for me; *I* knew nothing of it.' He is speaking here of his earlier childhood reading.

Chapter VIII
Never Wonder. The keynote of the Gradgrind philosophy is 'Never wonder', but stick rigidly to hard facts. In their room Tom and Louisa discuss Sissy and other topics: they consider the future, when Tom is to go into Bounderby's bank, hoping to enjoy himself there more than he has ever been able to at home. Louisa, for her part, is lost in thought, gazing at the fire, and is trying to control her wandering thoughts when, again, this time by her mother, she is told never to wonder.

Exactly half-way through Book the First Dickens writes what may be called a bridging chapter: firstly, it develops the relationship of the two older children; then, it repeats and re-emphasises the Fancy versus Fancy theme, and also appears to indicate that Sissy is having some softening beneficent effect upon the Gradgrind household. Quite clear too is the notion that Tom is thinking of using Bounderby's attachment to Louisa for his (Tom's) own advantage: this is to be a vital element of the unfolding plot. As mentioned in the section on Structure, this chapter marks the beginning of the original issue of the second month's division of the weekly serial publication: hereafter the novel, still tightly planned in great detail, can break new ground.

political economy Now generally called economics: the study or science of the production, distribution and consumption of wealth.

transported This system of punishment for crime by removing criminals to some penal settlement abroad dates, in England, from Elizabeth I's Vagrancy Act. At this time, as readers of *Great Expectations* will know, many convicts were transported to Australia. It was abolished in 1853.

De Foe Alternative spelling of Defoe: Daniel Defoe (about 1659–1731) was an English author and Dissenter, with some 375 publications attributed to him. The most celebrated, of course, is *Robinson Crusoe*, another of Dickens's favourite novels.

Euclid Euclides (about 300 BC), a noted Greek geometrician. Note the contrast between the romance and imagination of Defoe with the strict logic of the scientific geometrician.

Goldsmith Oliver Goldsmith (1728–74), an Irish writer who settled in London in 1756, and is celebrated principally for his poem *The Deserted Village*, his novel *The Vicar of Wakefield*, and the play *She Stoops to Conquer*.

Cocker Edward Cocker (1631–75) published an arithmetic textbook which ran through sixty editions. 'According to Cocker' thenceforth meant 'according to established rules and what is known to be correct'. Note again the contrast between imagination and fantasy, and scientific exactitude.

looking at the bright sparks Several of Dickens's characters are fascinated by the thoughtful, imaginative pursuit of gazing into the fire, among them Lizzie Hexham in *Our Mutual Friend*, Alice Brown in *Dombey and Son*, Redlaw in *The Haunted Man*, and John Perrybingle in *The Cricket on the Hearth*.

presses Cupboards and bookcases.

calcination The process of subjecting a material to the effect of prolonged heating at high temperatures.

calorification The production of heat, especially in living animal bodies.

Chapter IX
Sissy's Progress. Sissy Jupe, believing that her father will one day return, tolerates the fact-finding and fact-grinding establishments of Stone Lodge and the school, but her 'educational' progress is slow. She discusses the schooling with Louisa, and talks of her circus-clown father, whom she dearly loves. She constantly looks forward to a letter from him which never comes.

This is a run-of-the-mill chapter which emphasises what little 'progress' Sissy has in fact achieved either at school or in the Gradgrind household. However, it suggests a growing understanding between the two girls from such widely different backgrounds, and sketches in minor traits of personality in the Gradgrind family.

'To do unto others ... do unto me' Part of the Answer in the Church Catechism to the question: 'What is thy duty towards thy neighbour?' The Answer begins: 'My duty towards my neighbour is to love him as myself, and to do to all men as I would they should do unto me ...'

blue book Parliamentary or Privy Council report.

Sultan ... story A reference to the *Arabian Nights Entertainments*, the Arabic title more literally rendered, 'The Thousand Nights and a Night'. The Sultan Schahriar, convinced of the faithlessness of women, resolves to take a new wife every night and to have her slain the next morning. Scheherazade voluntarily becomes his wife, and by the telling of the tales wins respite from day to day, until after a thousand and one nights she wins her own security and changes the Sultan's views.

number one Oneself (slang).

Revision questions on Chapters V–IX

1 Detail all you have gathered about Sissy Jupe and her background: why does Mr Gradgrind take charge of her?

2 What sort of place is Coketown? Which English town or towns of today, in your opinion, are similar? How do its people occupy themselves when not at work?

3 What is Mr Sleary's 'philosophy' of life?

4 What is Bounderby's (*a*) real, (*b*) assumed attitude to Mrs Sparsit? In what ways is she either likeable or unlikeable?

5 'Never Wonder': how did this expression come to be the keynote of the young Gradgrinds' existence?

6 What further information has been provided of Sissy's background and upbringing in these chapters?

Chapter X
Stephen Blackpool. Forty-year-old Stephen Blackpool is a hard-working factory hand, a power-loom weaver, 'a man of

perfect integrity'. Walking home from work he meets Rachael who, over the years, has comforted him as an old friend in all his troubles and perplexities. They walk to Rachael's house together: he moves on to his, and finds there his wife, a drunken, debauched woman who periodically descends upon him in this wretched state to disturb and disrupt his life.

The second paragraph of this chapter is one extended sentence culminating in the name of a new character, soon to be linked with yet another: the workman hand-weaver of forty and a factory-hand working woman of about thirty-five from the same mill owned by Bounderby. Both are making their ways home through a typical 'Victorian' working-class scene of dark, ill-lit, wet, narrow streets with tightly-packed, small, terraced houses mostly let off in tiny flats. Blackpool's low spirits are deepened by the presence at home of his errant, abusive and dissolute drunken wife.

Titanic Gigantic, from the mythological Greek Titans of enormous size and strength, typical of lawlessness and the power of force.

Chapter XI
No Way Out. During the midday break of the following day Stephen Blackpool calls on his employer, Mr Bounderby, to ask his advice. He wants to know if and how he can be legally separated from his wife: they have been married nineteen years, but soon after marriage she went downhill, and she returns at random intervals drunken and penniless. Mr Bounderby, with Mrs Sparsit in self-righteous support, informs him that only a thousand pounds or more could effect such a separation: otherwise nothing can be done. Blackpool is disturbed, and wishes he were dead; Bounderby harangues him, telling him that he is turning, or is being led, into dangerous paths.

After the night, the day: after the misery and near-squalor of their homes, the 'Hands' are subjected to the unremitting toil, noise and heat of the mill. The opening few paragraphs

register Dickens's powerful indictment of laissez-faire industrialism and in particular its human exploitation, a theme
mirrored by the encounter between the 'man of perfect integrity' (Chapter X) and the outrageous Bounderby, who
assumes a high moral stance on the subject of divorce. Here
Dickens exposes a classic 'Victorian' attitude of hypocrisy,
with one law for the rich and none at all for the poor.

curse of all that tribe The serpent who tempted Eve in the
  Garden of Eden was punished by God: 'Upon thy belly shalt
  thou go, and dust shalt thou eat all the days of thy life'
  (Genesis, iii. 14).
netting A form of stitching, like that, though on a smaller scale,
  used by fishermen in constructing their nets. Perhaps she was
  making the mittens mentioned in the text: the stirrup on the
  foot was to hold and keep taut the loose thread and completed
  work.
dree Wearisome, tiresome.
played old Gooseberry Played the very deuce or devil.
brigg Bridge (north country form of the word).
fewtrills Little things or trifles (a dialect and provincial term).
hottering Vibrating, trembling (Scots).
Doctor's Commons Society or college of English lawyers, of
  considerable antiquity: its members, who had to be doctors of
  law of either Oxford or Cambridge, had the right of appearing
  in ecclesiastical, divorce, probate and admiralty courts. The
  college was dissolved in 1857. Dickens reported its proceedings,
  beginning there before he was seventeen: he often satirised its
  procedures in his works, notably in *David Copperfield*.

Chapter XII
The Old Woman. On leaving Bounderby's house Blackpool is
accosted by an old lady, who asks him if he has seen Mr
Bounderby, and wants to know of his health and well-being.
She accompanies him to the factory, chatting about her visit
to the town: she tells him that she comes annually just to catch
a glimpse of Bounderby. A little perplexed at all this Stephen
goes into work, and the old lady stands outside, watching as if
fascinated. At the end of the day Stephen waits for Rachael in
vain: he walks the streets in the cold rain, thinking of what

could have been his life had he married, or could marry Rachael: thoughtful and depressed, he turns for home.

A curious encounter, this. Stephen Blackpool, after having been bludgeoned by Bounderby's heartless pomposity, deserves solace and consolation which comes in part, oddly enough, from this unexpected hand on his arm from an un-known, un-named elderly visitor from the country asking detailed personal questions about Bounderby. More is learnt of Blackpool's long and deep, though chaste, relationship with Rachael, and of his wretched and apparently unbreakable bond with his drink-sodden wife.

hummobee A humming bee, often called a humble- or bumble-bee.
full-stop From its shape and appearance.
Parliamentary The Parliamentary Train, a type of railway service formerly operating in the United Kingdom. The railways were obliged, by the Regulation Act of 1844, to run at least one train a day over their particular region, at a minimum average speed of 12 m.p.h., calling at every station, at a fare not exceeding one penny a mile. The Act was repealed in 1915: the service had in fact ceased in 1912.
Divine Right Historically, the notion that kings reign by direct ordinance of God, quite apart from the will of the people.
Towers of Babel The reference is to Genesis, xi: the 'tower' was probably more pyramidal than cylindrical.

Chapter XIII
Rachael. Arriving home, Stephen finds Rachael there, tend-ing his wife: the room is tidied. He dozes off and dreams: he wakes to see his wife, craving for drink, take up the bottle of poison with which Rachael has been dressing her wounds. At the critical moment, Rachael starts up, and averts the danger. She has to leave, as it is early morning: Stephen hopes that one day, even in death perhaps, he and Rachael may be together.

Directly run-on from the previous chapter, this concen-trates on Rachael's compassion for both Blackpool and his wretched (and now injured) wife. It is bitterly ironic that Rachael should have been responsible for saving her life.

Rather theatrically, perhaps (and Dickens loved the theatre as playwright, actor and manager) and with a touch of sentimentality, the strained calm within the small room is contrasted with the surging storm of the elements outside. Stephen's nightmare reflects the confusion, desperation and helplessness of his tormented existence.

'Let him who is without sin ... stone at her!' A slightly modified version of John, viii. 7.
there is a deep gulf set See Luke, xvi. 19–31.
save my soul alive See Ezekiel, xviii. 27. The complete line is used as the first of the Opening Sentences at Morning and at Evening Prayer in the Church Liturgy.

Revision questions on Chapters X–XIII

1 Describe the relationship of Stephen and Rachael.

2 Why does Stephen go to Mr Bounderby about Mrs Blackpool? What, in brief, does his employer tell him?

3 What do you suspect about the old woman, and why?

4 As far as you can, explain Blackpool's dream.

Chapter XIV
The Great Manufacturer. Time passes, and Mr Gradgrind notices that his daughter Louisa is becoming a young woman, and that his son Tom is a young man: he is sent off to work at Bounderby's bank. Sissy (still hoping for her father's return) is acknowledged as a good, pleasant young woman who, regrettably, will never make progress in the practical system of Mr and Mrs M'Choakumchild's educational process. Time too sees Mr Gradgrind elected as M.P. for Coketown. Tom brings news that Mr Bounderby and their father are discussing serious matters at the Bank.

After four chapters involving Stephen Blackpool Dickens returns to the main plot, using the digression as an (impossibly long) interval. He has, therefore, perhaps a little creakingly, beguiled his readers into believing that several years have passed. Tom is now old enough to shave and pursue his selfish 'number one' endeavours in Bounderby's bank. Sissy now works in Bounderby's mill, still hoping her father is alive and will return. Gradgrind is now an M.P. for the locality. Louisa still stares at the glowing coals. In this rather strained way, forced on, doubtless, by the pressures of the serial form, Dickens hopes to persuade his readers that his characters have grown up, but not necessarily matured or overmuch changed, except perhaps for Louisa, whose private thoughts and emotions seem to have intensified. All this process has been economically accomplished in a short space.

bottle Of nine oils (see Chapters V–VI).
confab Colloquial abbreviation for confabulation – a familiar chat.

Chapter XV
Father and Daughter. Mr Gradgrind talks to Louisa in his study, telling her that Bounderby wishes to marry her, despite the disparity of their ages, which Gradgrind counteracts with copious and universal statistics. Louisa accepts the proposal, but betrays no love for her suitor: she tells her father that his system has suppressed any love and affection she might have had, which Gradgrind accepts as a complimentary testimonial to its efficacy. Mrs Gradgrind is pleased, as far as she can be; and Sissy is emotionally affected at Louisa's passive acceptance.

This longer chapter reveals the basic conflict between Fact and Fancy, which Louisa feels intensely but has not yet seen through, notwithstanding Sissy's influence. Gradgrind, despite earlier traces of possible mellowing, still cannot understand and certainly will not accept any faults in or changes to the 'system'. The paragraph beginning 'Why, father, she pursued ...' sums up to perfection her insight and emotional turbulence, while to her father it remains a tribute to his utilitarian principles and their success. The final paragraph of the chapter is equally significant: this is another issue which Dickens must resolve as his story moves on.

Blue Beard Usually Bluebeard, after Perrault's fairy-tale of
Barbe Bleue, 1697: a wealthy ruffian marries and kills six wives
one after the other, hanging up their remains in a locked
chamber: the horrible secret is discovered by the seventh wife.
The story is old in folk lore, and the name, quite naturally, has
been popularly applied to men notorious for monstrous crimes
against women.

Blue Books Parliamentary or Privy Council reports, bound with
blue covers.

round numbers Indefinite or approximate statements of a
number. In Chapter III we are told that Louisa is 'fifteen or
sixteen', and in Chapter IV that Bounderby is 'seven or eight
and forty'. 'Time went on in Coketown' (Chapter XIV), and
Louisa is 'in round numbers' now twenty. This would make
Bounderby 52 or 53. The man of Fact seems (deliberately?)
ambiguous here.

Calmucks of Tartary Properly Kalmuck, a people of Mongol
origin; many tribes remain in East Russia, China and Tibet.
Tartary is a vague term for the region between the Pacific and
the Dnieper.

utilitarian Based on usefulness alone, without regard to beauty
or pleasantness. Utilitarianism was an ethical doctrine that
actions are right in proportion to their usefulness or as they aim
to promote happiness: the end and criterion of public action is
'the greatest happiness of the greatest number'.

Chapter XVI
Husband and Wife. After much effort Mr Bounderby informs
Mrs Sparsit of his intended marriage: she wishes him happiness, almost pityingly. She is not to lose her post, but is to be
transferred to comfortable quarters at the Bank, maintaining
her independence. The marriage takes place, after which
Bounderby makes a pompous and egotistical speech, and the
pair leave for a honeymoon. Tom alone is elated at the turn of
events.

The First Book 'Sowing' ends here: Dickens has to move
fast to complete the foundations, so he pushes on quickly and
compresses a great deal of crucial material, beginning with
what seemed likely to be the great difficulty of Bounderby's
encounter with Mrs Sparsit over his impending marriage. It is

clear that her apparent goodwill and easy acceptance of change is to be a factor in, and a foretaste of, her eventual deeper involvement in the plot. Typically, Bounderby at the wedding breakfast, in claiming he is above making a speech, of course does so, proclaiming (once more) the squalor of his origins and his many virtues: the wily Tom has the last word, revelling in the likelihood of 'looking after number one' even more favourably from now on.

annual compliment A delightful genteelism. Dickens despised the subservient snobbery of the middle-class.

bread of dependence A coined phrase on the model of others of the Bible: Bread of Wickedness (Proverbs, iv. 17); Bread of Sorrows (or Carefulness), in Psalm cxxviii; and Bread of Idleness (Proverbs, xxxi. 27).

sweetbread The pancreas (sometimes the thymus) of animals, especially when used as food.

Lyons A city of France on the confluence of the Rhone and Saône, generally considered to be the second industrial centre of France, noted chiefly for its silk manufacture.

Revision questions on Chapters XIV–XVI

1 What indications are there of a better, more humane side to Mr Gradgrind's nature?

2 What is Tom's relationship with his sister? Do you feel it to be sincere or hypocritical?

3 Why does Louisa's attitude to Sissy undergo a change? What, do you consider, does each girl think of the marriage?

4 How does Mrs Sparsit take the news of Mr Bounderby's forthcoming marriage? What is Tom's reaction, and why?

Book the Second. Reaping

Chapter I
Effects in the Bank. On a hot midsummer day, with Coketown reeking of engine-oil, Mrs Sparsit and Bitzer (now the Bank's

porter) talk of the day's news, and decide that the workers of Coketown are a wretched lot and that Mr Thomas Gradgrind is an idler and a waster. A young stranger calls at the Bank, and with a sophisticated careless and bored air asks to know where Mr Bounderby lives. He has been recommended by Mr Gradgrind, the local M.P., to contact him: in general conversation he is particularly surprised to learn how young Mrs Bounderby is.

This is probably the longest chapter of the entire novel, forming a complete issue of Dickens's serial on 27 May 1854: it opens with what is ostensibly a detailed description of Coketown on a sweltering midsummer's day, a year after the marriage of Bounderby and Louisa. The scene is structured first from a distant, and then from a closer view (like cinematic or TV 'zooming'). What must be noted, however, is the overall implication of threat. This is heightened not only by the arrival of a smooth-talking stranger but also by the actions of the local industrialists, who will lock out their 'hands' rather than improve their working conditions. Dickens has thus incorporated further touches of mystery and expectation into his plot, whetting his readers' interest at the opening of a fresh section of his serial.

simoon A hot suffocating desert wind.
spumous Foamy or scummy.
laid his head It was then the custom for servants to have their beds made every night with the head against the door of the safe or strong-room of the house or office.
truckle beds A low bed that can be wheeled and stored under another.
Lucifer Satan, who was cast down to the uttermost recesses of the pit. See Isaiah, xiv. 4, 12.
Sultan A further reference, doubtless, to the *Arabian Nights Entertainments*.

Chapter II
Mr James Harthouse. The stranger is Mr James Harthouse, a gentleman idler who has been recommended by his M.P.

brother to join the 'Hard Fact fellows'. He meets Bounderby, who amid his usual intimations of his own wretched origins, extols the smoky industry of Coketown. Harthouse meets Louisa Bounderby, and thinks her remarkably self-contained. They converse, and over dinner he notices that Louisa comes to life only when her brother Tom appears, somewhat belatedly. Harthouse mentally sums him up as a whelp.

There are some interesting aspects of viewpoint worth noticing here. Dickens makes the most of the opportunity to offer what seems to be his own opinion of the intelligent but blasé, ever-bored, totally unserious society parasites of the powerful 'upper class' in Parliament (and elsewhere) who can make fun of a railway disaster. Nevertheless Harthouse, who qualifies as such a drone, is shown to be perceptive and intelligent. He soon sees through the pomposity of Bounderby, and – much more significantly – accurately appraises Louisa's situation and, later, Tom's essential nature as a disagreeable, ill-bred, untrustworthy 'young pup'.

Graces In classical mythology the three Graces were the goddesses who bestowed beauty and charm and were themselves the embodiment of both. They were the three sisters Aglaia, Thalia and Euphrosyne.

cornet of Dragoons Formerly a fifth-commissioned officer in a cavalry troop, who carried the colours: the Dragoons were once armed with a carbine called a dragoon.

Turkey carpets Soft thick kinds of carpet.

English family This is the family of Russell, dating from the fifteenth century, and the family name of the Dukes of Bedford. Dickens knew Lord John Russell (1792–1878) quite well. The motto is 'che sara sara', the Italian for 'what will be will be'.

polonies and saveloys A polony is a dry sausage of partly-cooked meat; a saveloy is a highly-seasoned sausage, originally of brains.

Chapter III
The Whelp. Tom, despite 'the system', has grown up hypo-critical, selfish and without discipline. In Harthouse's hotel room, under the influence of wine and tobacco to which he is

really unused, yet assuming a man-of-the-world air, Tom proves himself to be an over-talkative, gullible hypocrite. He tells Harthouse how Louisa married Bounderby more or less to make his (Tom's) life easier and more pleasant. He tells Harthouse too of Louisa's introspection, and of 'the system', and of Mrs Sparsit's longstanding, but unrequited, devotion to Mr Bounderby.

Tom proves himself to be precisely what Harthouse has assumed, and what we have already deduced from previous incidents and references: a callow youth, despite his pretensions, certainly no match for the equally self-interested but much more worldly Harthouse. Their evening encounter is simultaneously amusing and ominous: the final paragraph tersely warns us of dire consequences of Tom's revelations and untrustworthy nature, maintaining the atmosphere of suspense as the story progresses.

caustic Properly, something that exerts a corroding or disintegrating action on the skin and flesh. Harthouse, goading Tom on, is suggesting that his remarks are strong and bitter.

'Verb neuter ... does not care' This is a strong reminder of the days when Grammar was studied in particular detail: it is clear that Dickens remembered his own days in the class-room.

Revision Questions on Chapters I–III

1 What do Mrs Sparsit and Bitzer think of Tom Gradgrind?

2 Describe the physique and character of James Harthouse so far as revealed in these chapters. Why should he be so curious about Louisa Bounderby?

3 What does Harthouse learn from 'The Whelp'? How much of it do we know to be true?

Chapter IV
Men and Brothers At a union meeting Slackbridge, a violent agitator for a combined and total union of all the local work-

people, forces Stephen Blackpool to be 'sent to Coventry' by his workmates. Blackpool is summoned by Bitzer to Bounderby's house.

Dickens presents the Union official unsympathetically, almost in caricature, commenting adversely on his appearance, physique, honesty and integrity. Stockbridge is apparently no more humane than the employers whose oppression and exploitation he is attacking. Yet there is something unconvincing here. Only one 'hand' stand against the Union's fundraising scheme and the unvoted-for and unspecified injunctions. Why should such sympathy as there was for Blackpool evaporate so quickly, and his being 'sent to Coventry' arouse no dissent? However, Stephen's role in the novel has not yet been played out and Dickens, for reasons yet to be revealed, feels the need to stress Blackpool's isolation.

sold his birthright This refers to Esau. See Genesis, xxv. 24–6, 34.

Judas Iscariot One of the Apostles of Christ, who afterwards betrayed Him to the priests for a bribe of thirty pieces of silver. See Matthew, xxvi. 1–56; Mark, xiv. 43–6; Luke, xxii. 1–48.

Castlereagh Robert Stewart, Viscount Castlereagh (1769–1822), a British statesman who invoked criticism and resentment for his policies in Ireland during the rising of 1798; the so-called Peterloo massacre (in which the military fired on a workmen's meeting in Manchester, 16 August 1819); and the Six Acts. His long-clouded reputation has recently been reconsidered, and a juster estimate of his statesmanship prevails.

hetter Heated, a dialect and provincial word.

moydert From a dialect word (usually spelt moider or moither), meaning confused, overcome, stupefied.

fratch Quarrel or brawl (provincial word).

Roman Brutus This is not Marcus Junius Brutus (85–42 BC), Caesar's general and assassin (among others of the Cassius conspiracy), but Lucius Junius Brutus, who roused the Romans to expel the Tarquin family (about 509 BC). He did indeed put to death his own sons for attempting to restore the Tarquins.

Spartan mothers Sparta, one of the leading city-states of Greece, was a military state noted for its courage and stern discipline: the term Spartan denotes one who can bear great pain without flinching. It was the Spartan mother who, handing her son the shield he was to carry into battle, told him to return either with it or on it.

fugleman A ringleader or mouthpiece of others.

Chapter V
Men and Masters. In the presence of Bounderby and his wife, Tom and Mr Harthouse, Blackpool refuses to say anything about Slackbridge and the Union combination, or about his own refusal (other than that it was a promise) to join it, though he denies that the men are rebels or rascals. He tells Bounderby of the general confusion, monotony and lack of proper direction of the people's energies, and of their not sharing in the apparent prosperity of Coketown: in his own quiet way, he condemns the whole structure of 'laissez-faire' principles. Bounderby sacks him, knowing full well that this will mean Stephen's permanent unemployment in the industry.

This chapter neatly draws Stephen and Bounderby into the heart of the Bounderby household with Louisa, Tom and Harthouse all present and variously addressed and affected. Blackpool is not merely sacked: he has, because of his principles, honestly and harmlessly held, been rendered unemployable through the 'old boy' confederation of the employers. A glimmer of hope remains (alas not for him): he seems to find only Louisa sympathetic. Could this mean that she has been moved by his plight, and can feel genuine compassion?

card Process wool (or raise the nap on cloth) by a comb-like apparatus.
shipped off to penal settlements See note on 'transported', p. 28.
Norfolk Island An islet in the Pacific, 400 miles north-west of New Zealand and 930 miles north-east of Sydney, and belonging to Australia since 1914. Convicts were sent here in the eighteenth and nineteenth centuries.
likens Likings.

Chapter VI
Fading Away. As he leaves Bounderby's house Stephen encounters Rachael and the old woman (see Chapter XII) who

calls herself Mrs Pegler and is on another visit to Coketown, this time especially to see Bounderby's wife. Stephen tells Rachael of his dismissal, and they all go back to his lodgings to eat, where Mrs Pegler talks vaguely of her past life and her lost son. People are announced, and Mrs Pegler, quite scared at the name of Bounderby, retreats into a corner when Mrs Bounderby and her brother Tom arrive. Louisa wants to help. It transpires that it is to Rachael that Blackpool made his irrevocable promise not to be involved in disputes; he grace-fully accepts some money from Louisa. On their departure, Tom delays a moment, telling Blackpool privately that he too might be able to help him if he would wait outside the Bank a while for a message. Blackpool takes leave of Rachael, works out his time, leaves, waits unavailingly outside the Bank, and finally makes his way out of Coketown, looking back at it from a distance.

In this longer chapter, the first of three to be complete Saturday instalments running consecutively, it is confirmed that Louisa has moved some distance from barren facts to at least a glimpse of reality (and we recall her and Tom as children peeping through the circus fence, and beginning to wonder). For the first time she speaks directly to members of the working-class: such was (and perhaps still is to some extent) the gulf between rich and poor. We are also left wondering what is the true relationship between Mrs Pegler and Bounderby, and what Tom is up to in asking Stephen to wait outside the Bank after work. Dickens still has, in the popular phrase, several cards up his sleeve! (He was, in fact, a very accomplished amateur conjuror.)

leetsome Gay, lively, cheering.
Lord Chesterfield Philip Dormer Stanhope, 4th Earl of Chesterfield (1694–1773), statesman, orator and wit, is also remembered as a letter-writer to his natural son Philip Stanhope, his letters containing much worldly wisdom. He received the celebrated letter from Dr Johnson (1755), who earlier in life had unavailingly awaited Chesterfield's patronage.

he saw land A curious expression meaning, from the context, that he saw the end of his time (of work) approaching, as the sailor, once in sight of land, knows that his voyage is all but over.

Chapter VII
Gunpowder. In his desultory fashion Harthouse makes headway among the 'Hard Facts' fraternity, and is increasingly interested in the hidden and pent-up emotions of Louisa Bounderby, who lives now at her husband's newly-acquired property in the countryside outside Coketown. Harthouse talks to Louisa in the woods near the house, mainly about her brother's gambling, and Louisa's obvious help with his debts; also mentioned are the defects of the Gradgrind educational system. Tom himself arrives: later, alone with Harthouse, Tom confesses to an extreme boredom, and to borrowing heavily from his sister, revealing extreme and callous inconsiderateness. Soon after, however, once Harthouse has offered his help and advice, he tells Louisa of his fondness for her. This delights her enormously and, as it appears linked with Harthouse's influence, seems to have softened somewhat her attitude towards Harthouse himself.

This long chapter is a particularly careful piece of exposition. It reveals subtle but perceptible changes of relationship and attachment impelled by Harthouse's languid but intelligent appraising of a developing situation. He has 'designs' on Louisa: she betrays confidences of her being used by her brother, who is outwitted by Harthouse at every turn. Indeed Tom, too, like his sister, is becoming more aware of attitudes alien to his utilitarian and selfish upbringing. A dangerous trail of metaphorical gunpowder is being laid in the leafy countryside retreat: the lightest spark will cause immense damage with long-term and possibly irreversible consequences.

polite deadly sins The stock seven Deadly or Capital sins are: Pride, Wrath, Envy, Lust, Gluttony, Avarice, Sloth.
Gorgon In classical mythology the Gorgons or Gorgones were three frightful maidens, Stheno, Euryale and Medusa, all with

hissing serpents for hair, and with wings, brazen claws and enormous teeth. Medusa's head was so fearful that those who looked upon it were changed to stone.

depth answers unto depth A variant of Psalm xlii. 7, 'Deep calleth unto deep'.

foreclosed a mortgage In law, foreclosure is the process by which a mortgagor, having failed to repay the money lent on the security of an estate, is compelled to forfeit his right to redeem the estate.

shaving himself in a boot Shaving himself in his reflection of a well-polished boot. Dickens is recollecting one of the advertisements of the blacking factory in the Strand where he had worked as a twelve-year-old.

Westminster School An English public school originating in a school attached to Westminster Abbey and refounded by Henry VIII and then again by Elizabeth in 1560. Boys who gain scholarships on the Elizabethan foundation are known as king's scholars, and they have the privilege of election to studentships at Christ Church, Oxford and to scholarships at Trinity College, Cambridge.

Arcadian proceeding Arcadia or Arcady was a district in Greece whose people were primitive in manners, and given to music and dancing: the adjective thus means pastoral, simple or innocent.

of the world worldly An adaptation of the Biblical: 'The first man is of the earth, earthy' (1 Corinthians, xv. 47).

Familiar A spirit or demon supposed to attend a person at call.

Revision questions on Chapters IV–VII

1 Why and how is Blackpool 'sent to Coventry' by his workmates? What is Mr Bounderby's reaction?

2 What new information do we gain from and about the old woman (Mrs Pegler)? Why is she so startled at the prospect of meeting Mrs Bounderby?

3 What happens at Blackpool's rooms between Louisa, Tom and Blackpool?

4 How did Bounderby obtain his country house?

5 What does Harthouse tell Louisa about her brother? What are his personal opinions of 'The Whelp', and why?

Chapter VIII
Explosion. Next day Harthouse reflects pleasurably on his successful beginnings with Louisa. Returning to the house, he is surprised by an outraged Bounderby, who informs him that the Bank has been robbed with a false key of over a hundred pounds, taken from Tom's safe. Bounderby is rudely impatient with the Bank servants, Mrs Sparsit and Bitzer, and suspects Stephen Blackpool. Later, Mrs Sparsit, temporarily resident at the Bounderby home so as to recover from the shock, affects pity and solace for her employer. Very early in the morning Louisa creeps to Tom's room, and they discuss the day's events: on her departure, Tom is in a mixed and very disturbed mood.

In different ways the Bank robbery (of a paltry sum) brings together physically – or at least under suspicion – Louisa, Bounderby, Harthouse, Mrs Sparsit, Tom, Blackpool and Mrs Pegler: a neat integration of hitherto outspread themes. Mrs Sparsit seizes the golden and long-awaited opportunity to regain her previous status in Bounderby's new home, and by various tactics, to try to dominate him and Louisa and affect their relationship to her own advantage.

brimstone Sulphur. The alchemists looked upon it as the principle of fire, and it has long associations with 'Hell-fire'.
Dutch clocks Clocks of wood and wire with brass wheels, made in the Black Forest, and properly 'deutsch' (German) clocks. The whirring sound preceding the strike is often louder in these clocks than in others.
'Alas poor Yorick!' The King of Denmark's dead jester, 'a fellow of infinite jest and most excellent fancy', over whose skull Hamlet meditates in Shakespeare's play of that name (V. i).
candles were brought Illuminating gas was known in the late eighteenth century, and by the early years of the nineteenth Pall Mall, Westminster Bridge, and the Streets of Westminster were lit by gas, the fore-runner of the Gas Light and Coke Co. being established in 1812. Candles, however, remained in use for some time as cheaper, and involving less work than the oil-lamp.
backgammon A game for two persons, played on a board with dice and fifteen men or pieces each.

Chapter IX
Hearing the Last of It. Mrs Sparsit eagerly watches all the activities of the house, and prowls about endlessly, sounding out all and sundry, and provoking friction between the uncouth Bounderby and his quiet passive wife, thus throwing Louisa and Harthouse more on each other's company. Bitzer brings a note to say that Mrs Gradgrind is very ill, and Louisa returns hastily, yet unemotionally, to her old home. Her mother is tended by Sissy, and, in her dying wanderings, realises, after all and at last, that something valuable was missing from her children's lives.

Mrs Sparsit is succeeding in installing herself as mistress of Bounderby's country retreat, but the emphasis here is on one of Dickens's specialities, a death scene. This, of Mrs Gradgrind's passing, is handled with supreme control and sensitivity, following a long paragraph 'Neither, as she approached ... figs and thistles', of exquisite power, evocation and balance. Sissy's beneficent effect upon Jane is significantly recorded, and one awaits with interest some clear signs of positive rapprochement between Louisa and Sissy Jupe.

grapes ... thistles From Matthew, vii. 16.
man walketh and disquieteth himself From the Prayer Book version of the thirty-ninth Psalm, used in the Order for The Burial of the Dead.

Chapter X
Mrs Sparsit's Staircase. Mrs Sparsit remains at Bounderby's house for a while and is, indeed, invited by Bounderby to stay there every weekend: she pictures Louisa Bounderby as descending a staircase towards shame and ruin, and enjoys imagining her eventual discomfiture. Bounderby awaits news of the robbery: Louisa and Mr Harthouse discuss the crime; and Mrs Sparsit waits too, watching Louisa's descent.

The second paragraph of the previous chapter introduced the notion of an allegorical Staircase, developed in the third paragraph here, by which Mrs Sparsit 'with consummate velocity' spies on the household, especially Louisa. The metaphorical image, of course, also applies especially to Mrs Sparsit's expectation of Louisa's irreversible descent into an immoral relationship with Harthouse.

clover i.e. luxury or abundance.

feeding on the fat of the land i.e. living extremely well. The allusion is Biblical (see Genesis, xlv. 18).

'To hear is to obey' Commonly repeated injunction of the *Arabian Nights* tales, in various forms (e.g. 'Hearkening and obedience', 'I heard and obey the commands of . . .').

Romulus and Remus In ancient Roman legend the twin sons of Mars and Rhea Silvia, and the legendary founders of Rome. According to the old tale the children were ordered to be drowned in the Tiber, but were miraculously saved, and suckled by a she-wolf.

a regular Alderney The Alderney is a small dairy-cow, formerly of a breed kept in Alderney, the most northerly of the Channel Islands.

under the rose From the Latin expression *sub rosa*, implying some confidence, or communication in confidence, under the pledge of secrecy, of which the rose was an emblem.

Chapter XI
Lower and Lower. Mrs Sparsit remains on the alert: Bounderby has to go away on business, but she is to spend her weekends at the house as usual. She learns from Tom that Mr Harthouse too is away, and that he is to meet Tom at Coketown station the next day. Mrs Sparsit remains at the Bank on the Saturday, and later furtively hangs about the station watching Tom awaiting Harthouse's arrival. He does not come, and Mrs Sparsit triumphantly concludes that he is with Louisa. She rushes away, reaching the house and creeping about until she hears the low voices of Louisa and Harthouse in close conversation. Apparently they are to meet again that night. It begins to rain heavily: Mrs Sparsit sees Louisa leave the house, and she follows her to the station, but loses sight of her at Coketown itself.

Mrs Sparsit, resident at Bounderby's bank except at the week-ends, maintains her vigilant surveillance, by whatever means, of Louisa's movements and activities. Her frenzied pursuit borders on the ridiculous, but it is nevertheless menacing: she means to destroy Louisa's reputation and marriage (indeed Louisa seems on the verge of accomplishing this for herself). Mrs Sparsit revels, almost fiendishly, and despite the thunderstorm, in the prospect of catching out Louisa in the very act of marital infidelity, a hint of voyeurism – a deliberate secretive observation of another's private, usually sexual, behaviour.

apostrophizing Addressing someone (or something) as would a poet or an orator.

small fry The less important, here the less significant beings in his employment.

walnut ketchup A sauce made from walnuts.

India ale A variety of beer brewed for consumption in India, so as not to deteriorate in the climate there, and later sold on the English market.

furies The Roman name for the avenging goddesses of Greek mythology: winged deities of terrible appearance who avenged crimes, especially of kinship.

Robinson Crusoe The hero of Defoe's romance of the same name (published in 1719). The shipwrecked Crusoe, with infinite ingenuity, accustoms himself to life on a desert island. We know that Dickens was much taken with the book when very young.

Chapter XII
Down. At home Mr Gradgrind is disturbed at his work by the arrival of a distraught Louisa, who upbraids him bitterly as having been, however unwittingly, the cause of her extreme unhappiness: so reared, educated and married off without sentiment and feeling, the declaration of Harthouse as her lover has brought her near to disgrace, although, in fact, she has not been compromised. This is the culmination and consequence of the Gradgrind system. She faints away at her father's feet.

This short chapter concludes Book the Second: the world of statistics, -ologies, never wondering, the system, has come full circle as the cause, and in the bitterness of Louisa's wild despair, she cannot handle, and is emotionally incapable of handling, her moral dilemma. Gradually, in what must be considered a rather theatrical scene (Dickens was intensely interested in theatre as playwright and actor-manager) Gradgrind responds. The result is an initial stripping away of his utilitarian dogmas: at long last they have been eroded by natural instinct.

Good Samaritan Read the parable in Luke, x. 29–37.

Revision Questions on Chapters VIII–XII

1 Why is Louisa so affected by the news of the Bank robbery? How was the robbery accomplished? Why is Blackpool immediately suspected?

2 What do we learn, and from whom, of the relationship between Louisa and her husband?

3 For what is Mrs Sparsit so eagerly looking? Why? What is her 'staircase'?

4 Give an account of the last moments of Mrs Gradgrind. Does Dickens create any sympathy with her?

5 Why does Louisa return to her father? What circumstances led up to that moment? What is Mr Gradgrind's reaction? What does he learn of himself?

Book the Third. Garnering

Chapter I
Another Thing Needful. Louisa awakens in her old room: she has been tended by Sissy, who has had a wholesome and cheering effect on the house and the Gradgrind youngsters. Gradgrind himself comes in and confesses himself stunned by the failure and inadequacy of the cherished system. Later Louisa and Sissy talk together: they now understand each other thoroughly.

The First Chapter of Book I was entitled 'The One Thing Needful': what was offered was nothing but Facts and all that implied. Now, neatly devised, the first chapter of the last Book aptly reminds us that something else is necessary, not only to have a feeling, open mind and heart but also to surrender to one's discovered reality, unashamedly to give way to one's feelings, and to respect the feelings of others. This was the core of Louisa's intense struggle to free herself from all those years of conditioning, of emotional restriction and suppression. Only Sissy's consoling presence and calm influence, her natural gift of understanding, can heal wounds, making 'girl number twenty' a crucial element in the garnering or gathering-in of the threads of the story.

shadows of a dream Compare Keats's line in *Endymion*, 'A hope beyond the shadow of a dream'.
excise-rod Measuring-stick or gauge.

Chapter II
Very Ridiculous. An agitated Mr Harthouse is at a loss to know where Louisa is: Tom knows nothing helpful, and both Bounderby and Mrs Sparsit are away. Back at the hotel he is confronted by Sissy, who tells him that he will never see Louisa again, and that it would be better for him to leave Coketown. He does so, utterly defeated by her frankness and solicitude for Louisa.

Dickens has no further use for Harthouse once the 'conversion' of the Gradgrind household had been effected, mainly through Sissy's influence and intervention: of course we await to see what consequences this will have on the marriage. It may appear incredible that Harthouse yields so readily to Sissy's (very polished and articulate) challenge: however, from a technical point of view there would be little value in extending an otherwise very tight story, knowing what we now know, and when other mysteries have yet to be cleared. Note how the words 'ridicule' and 'ridiculous' occur no fewer than six times in a comparatively short chapter: the once passive,

cowed, 'possessed of no facts' (Book I, Chapter ii) Sissy Jupe
dominates the scene.

in the Lancashire manner There are various local rules governing
  wrestling, and the Lancashire style (known as the 'catch-as-catch-
  can') is a popular free style, in which any hold is allowed.
Holy Office and slow torture A reference to the Holy
  Inquisition of the Catholic Church, in which, from the thirteenth
  century, heresy or suspected heresy was suppressed with
  terrifying ruthlessness.
gallery This would be a long balcony surrounding the inn-yard,
  a typical feature of the traditional coaching-inns.

Chapter III
Very Decided. Mrs Sparsit, full of what she believes to be the
true story of Louisa and Mr Harthouse, pursues Bounderby to
London, telling him all she knows before swooning off. They
return to Coketown. At Stone Lodge they meet Mr Gradgrind, who refutes all Mrs Sparsit's insinuations by relating
the true facts. Mrs Sparsit is discountenanced. Bounderby,
still selfish and pompous, cannot understand Gradgrind's ex-
planations, and insists on Louisa's returning to him by the
next day at noon, or he will not see her again. At five minutes
past twelve the next day he sends off Louisa's things, advertises
his country house, and resumes a bachelor life.

Structurally, this is an extremely important chaper: it inte-
grates themes previously worked over such as the ending of
Harthouse's role and the futility of Mrs Sparsit's frenzied
pursuit, and echoes the telling encounter between Bounderby
and Blackpool about the possibility of the latter's divorce
(Book I, Chapter xi). Even more significant is the masterful
presentation of a 'converted' Gradgrind, intimations of which
have been noted throughout the story: he presents a clear,
credible, unsentimental and unflurried case for tolerance,
understanding, feeling and sensitivity in human relationships.
It may be noted that Bounderby has the longer exchanges of
dialogue (that was always his selfish, pompous way), but
Gradgrind scores the greater effects. Bounderby on the

defensive is indeed hardened in his usual unchanging, un-compromising attitude: Gradgrind is impervious to his bluster, and emerges as a totally changed man, but his sufferings are not yet over.

St. James's Street A London thoroughfare connecting Piccadilly with Pall Mall: a famous street, with celebrated coffee-houses and clubs, among whose residents have been Byron, Gibbon, Thackeray and Wren. The precise hotel in which Bounderby stayed is, of course, unknown, and hardly matters.

Cock-and-a-Bull A cock and bull story is a long, rambling, idle or incredible yarn. Much ingenuity and research has been engaged on establishing the origin of the expression, which is still not conclusively known.

shoeing-horn An instrument of horn (or metal) for easing a shoe onto the foot.

rocket This could be the familiar explosive firework or military missile (of the day), or a reference to George Stephenson's (1781–1848) steam-engine of 1829.

pinch of candle-snuff A typical Bounderby expression: a boisterous and windy embellishment to a 'pinch of snuff', that is, a negligible quantity.

for better for worse Part of the Marriage Service.

Revision questions on Chapters I–III

1 What do we learn of Sissy's character and development in these chapters?

2 Why does James Harthouse leave Coketown? How is he affected by all that he has done or attempted?

3 What news does Mrs Sparsit convey to Mr Bounderby?

4 In what way or ways have Mr Gradgrind's views been changed?

5 Why and how does Mr Bounderby resume a bachelor's life?

Chapter IV
Lost. The pursuit of the bank robber continues: neither Stephen Blackpool nor the old lady can be traced. Bounderby

offers a reward for the discovery and arrest of Blackool, and Slackbridge (see II. iv) addresses a meeting referring to him as an example of dishonesty they are well rid of. At home Sissy tells Louisa of the arrival of Bounderby, Tom and Rachael; the working-woman gives an account of what happened on the night of Blackpool's departure (see II. vi). Rachael explains that Blackpool has had to change his name in order to find employment, and that he has promised to return within two days in order to clear himself of the charges laid against him. But he does not return; a week passes, and still he does not appear.

A bridging chapter, with a further indication, not entirely essential in the form expressed, of Dickens's suspicion of Trades Union tactics. Otherwise this is a summary of previous events, in part a gathering of loose ends, and a delaying tactic heightening the suspense over Blackpool's whereabouts and fate.

Venus Originally a Roman goddess of the spring, and later identified with the Greek Aphrodite: an important divinity in both religions and, as Aphrodite (the name means 'of the foam of the sea') goddess of love and beauty who sprang from the sea.
creeping on your bellies See note on 'curse of all that tribe', p. 31.

Chapter V
Found. Rachael, now befriended by Sissy, believes naturally and implicitly in Blackpool's integrity and honesty. They go out for a walk. Near Bounderby's house they see an agitated Mrs Sparsit bundling an old lady, none other than Mrs Pegler, out of a coach and into Mr Bounderby's house. Sissy and Rachael, and some bystanders and neighbours, crowd in, and Mr Bounderby, Mr Gradgrind and Tom appear. Mrs Sparsit produces the old woman as one connected with the robbery. Mrs Pegler turns out to be Bounderby's mother, who gives the complete lie to all Bounderby's stories of his early privations and treatment. He blusters absurdly, and the party disperses.

Rachael and Sissy, and particularly Louisa, have growing suspicions about the true culprit.

It is of course not Stephen Blackpool who has been found, as the chapter title would lead us to expect, but Josiah Bounderby who has been found out, and before irreproachable witnesses to his embarrassed humiliation. The 'mystery woman' element has been amusingly eased out of the plot, leaving the way clear for the final, crucial discovery of Stephen's (or another's) involvement in the Bounderby Bank robbery.

Slough of Despond In Bunyan's *Pilgrim's Progress* this is a deep bog which Christian has to cross: it has come to mean a period or fit of extreme depression and dejection.

Chapter VI
The Starlight. Sissy and Rachael walk in the country around Coketown, and find some broken fence-work, and then Blackpool's hat. To their horror, they discover that they are on the brink of an old pit-shaft, and Blackpool is doubtless lying at the bottom. They summon help to the Old Hell Shaft, and after long delays and great difficulties the maimed body of Stephen Blackpool is painfully raised to the surface. He tells his story brokenly: Rachael stays by his side, walking alongside his stretcher, comforting him. Before long he dies.

This episode begins in sunlight and ends in starlight, a feature which symbolises its content. The fourth paragraph mentions, as part of the landscape, the dangerous presence of old pit shafts: by the next thirty lines the 'lost' Blackpool has been found, and then follows the frenzied activity, told with immense power, passion and tension, of his rescue from the notorious Old Hell Shaft. At one fell swoop Dickens has cleared the Blackpool mystery: Stephen's brave, honest and poignant words just before his death yield enough clues for the resolution of the other unsolved puzzle, the bank robbery. The entire chapter is a masterpiece of scrupulous construction and changes of pace: the final paragraph is an excellent example of

Dickens's superb word-control added to the power of stark simplicity.

fire-damp Miner's name for carburetted hydrogen, explosive when mixed in certain proportions with air, and a constant menace in mines.

Revision questions on Chapters IV–VI

1 What does Slackbridge have to say about Blackpool's alleged actions and disappearance? Why need he mention him at all?

2 Why does Rachael intervene with Bounderby and Tom?

3 Describe the scene of Mrs Pegler's revelations. What effect have these on Mr Bounderby?

4 How is Blackpool eventually found?

Chapter VII
Whelp-Hunting. On Sissy's whispered instructions Tom disappears from the crowd around the Old Hell Shaft. Gradgrind realises his son's crime, and hears how Sissy has sent him to hide at Sleary's circus. There they all go, by varying routes so as to avert suspicion, and they meet Sleary, who reminisces, and who has disguised Tom as a black servant in his show. With Sleary's help Gradgrind intends to ship off his disgraced son, a bitter product of his system, but Bitzer arrives suddenly, and apprehends Tom.

We have now reached Dickens's final instalment, the twentieth, of his *Household Words* serial: this and the following two chapters completed his story on Saturday, 12 August 1854. The wheel begins to complete its full circle. The author's thorough pre-planning, coupled with his gifted sense of exquisite irony and his sharp eye for detail, effect this skilful turn of fate. The circus condemned by Gradgrind as degraded, a symbol of 'idleness and folly' (Book I, Chapter iii), has become the only instrument of Tom's escape from the severity of the law and for his family's avoidance of public disgrace.

down-wells Here meaning stair-wells, the space surrounded by stairways, especially in high buildings.
Bourne Goal.
postillion, who happened ... in a fly A postillion is (usually was) a rider on the near horse pulling a coach or carriage. Here this unpleasant driver is found kicking a horse drawing a fly, a one-horse hackney-carriage.
butcher Nursery rhyme, in riddle form (explained in text).

> Two legs sat upon three legs with one leg in his lap;
> In comes four legs, and runs away with one leg;
> Up jumps two legs, catches up three legs,
> Throws it after four legs,
> And makes him bring back one leg.

grown too maturely turfy He had grown a beard.
Athley'th Astley's, from Philip Astley (1742–1814), a celebrated English equestrian and circus manager. After serving with distinction in the Seven Years' War, he went round England giving exhibitions of horsemanship, in which his son later joined him. At various times he had amphitheatres in London, Dublin and Paris, including Astley's Royal Amphitheatre near Westminster Bridge, from 1774 until 1796. It had an extremely high standard of performance. We know that Dickens went there as a youth: it is mentioned in *The Old Curiosity Shop*, and was often recollected by Dickens in his later years in all its light, colour and excitement. A plaque marks the spot today.
jothkin Joskin, a clown or bumpkin in thieves' slang.

Chapter VIII
Philosophical. Bitzer, the perfection of the system, has orders to return with the suspected Tom to Coketown and Mr Bounderby. He is impervious to appeals to his better nature, which the system has successfully suppressed. Sleary, however, has a stratagem, involving an intelligent dog, which succeeds in getting Tom off to Liverpool. Later he tells Gradgrind that Jupe, Sissy's father, must be dead, as the dog Merrylegs returned to the circus to die. Sleary too has a philosophy of life, which he expounds to the humiliated Gradgrind.

The details of Tom's (perhaps undeserved?) escape are

presented in typical Dickensian style: a mixture of the grotesque, comedy blended with tragic overtones, the almost incredible rendered convincing – all related with verve, gusto and relish. Note the two animals who assisted the escape: the dancing horse takes us back to the schoolroom at the very beginning of the novel ('Girl number twenty unable to define a horse!') and the use of the resourceful dog which pinned down Bitzer (who could achieve a factual definition) leads Sleary into the solution of the one remaining 'mystery': the fate of Signor Jupe. The return of the faithful Merrylegs and his subsequent death asserts the demise of Sissy's father. Dickens has now tidied up all the significant strands of the past.

Harvey William Harvey (1578–1657) who published in 1628 his explanation of the circulation of the blood.
not reckoning Luth 'Lush' is a slang term for alcoholic liquor.

Chapter IX
Final. Still the egotist and blusterer, Bounderby packs off Mrs Sparsit to her relation Lady Scadgers, but not before his housekeeper speaks her mind about him. We are given a glimpse of the future: Mrs Sparsit and Lady Scadgers at loggerheads, Bounderby persistent until death (and after that, by his will) in his officiousness and pomposity, Mr Gradgrind pursuing a changed course after publicly exonerating Black- pool and accusing his own son. Tom is in fact to die abroad; Rachael works on, still helping the wretched wife of Black- pool; Louisa, herself alone, is to be happy in the love and friendship of Sissy and her children, helping a little to bring happiness and kindness into the world around her.

In a final chapter Dickens, using a conventional device of most Victorian novelists, provides a sequence of short prophetic vignettes, often in extended sentences, describing the fate of twelve of his major characters (no details, however, of the old woman, Mrs Pegler) but including Mrs Blackpool. For most, hard times are still to be endured, with fortitude. Only three, all women, are to find varying degrees of content, mostly through service to others, and kindness and tolerance to all: Dickens's persistent message to his readers throughout his major novels and much of his other writings.

Revision questions on Chapters VII–IX

1 Why and when does Sissy ensure Tom's escape? How is Gradgrind brought to realise his son's implication in the robbery?

2 Briefly compress Sleary's news about the fortunes of the circus and its troupe. What is his plan to help Tom's escape?

3 How is Bitzer prevented from 'arresting' Tom?

4 Give Mrs Sparsit's final summing-up of Mr Bounderby: how far is it justified?

5 What is to be the future life of Mrs Sparsit, Mr Gradgrind and Louisa?

The characters

Elsewhere in these Notes it is said that *Hard Times* is the shortest of Dickens's important works, that it was a serial published in weekly instalments, and that it was a patiently planned novel with a serious purpose. These factors naturally affect the style (for this, see separate section) and the characterisation. In 120,000 words or so, compared with, say, *Great Expectations* (189,000 words), *Pickwick Papers* (about 357,000 words), *Barnaby Rudge* (about 260,000 words) or *The Old Curiosity Shop* (about 220,000 words) there is necessarily little room to spare either for the expanded episode, the extended description or, what is particularly relevant here, the detailed delineation of character or the involvement of sundry people incidental to the main plot. Dickens's usually enormous canvases, drawn in detail with great embellishment and gusto, give way here to a closely-knit group of people in a limited, almost oppressively limited locality, and each of the dozen or so major characters, with each of the remaining dozen 'minor' characters, has a particular relevance and significance in the fabric of the story. *Pickwick* has over eighty characters (apart from those in the stories introduced); *Nicholas Nickleby* about one hundred and and forty; and there are nearly one hundred in *David Copperfield*. While such counts mean little in themselves, they do serve to emphasise the remarkable concentration, conciseness and interlocking nature of this story. The characters, consequently, are drawn starkly, boldly, graphically; their features, nature, eccentricities and development (where this is evident) are indicated sharply, without extraneous details. In the book in general not a word is wasted: and with the characters themselves every word about them is telling and positive. It is to be noted too that this is a novel of 'character', not of incident. The theme, a criticism of materialism and a plea for love and imagination in human relationships, is played out through the characters themselves, who therefore become symbolic in the process, each indicative of some feeling, passion or desire (good or bad, fulfilled or thwarted) known to exist in human society. They become not merely characters of a novel, but also and perhaps more importantly, symbols in a fable or allegory: the book is a plea, a message forced from the heart, and the characters are the agents through which Dickens hopes to reach and catch the humanity and Christian tolerance, the understanding tempered by charity, of his audience.

Another general point about characterisation is worth making, to be amplified later where necessary. The deliberate purposeful nature of the novel has another consequence apart from the conciseness and economy already mentioned: it tends to make certain characters, in their symbolism, into caricatures. It is difficult to imagine anyone, ever speaking as Bounderby or Gradgrind do, or even Stephen Blackpool or Slackbridge. In this connection G. B. Shaw remarks pertinently: '. . .Here he [Dickens] begins at last to exercise quite recklessly his power of presenting a character to you in the most fantastic and outrageous terms, putting into its mouth from one end of the book to the other hardly a word which could conceivably be uttered by any sane human being, and yet leaving you with an unmistakable and exactly truthful portrait of a character that you recognise at once as not only real but typical.'

A final point concerns the characters' names. Dickens knew well the strength of having a character aptly named: in *Hard Times* his deliberateness in this connection is highly marked and significant. Gradgrind: one for whom everything can be graduated and graded, who believes in grinding down his facts into all and sundry; Bounderby (Dickens toyed with Bound, then Bounder, and finally Bounderby) who *is* a bounder, obtrusively ill-bred, and ill-mannered, and is also bounded and limited by his beliefs, knowing many of them to be lies. The M'Choakumchilds need no explanation; Jupe has a foreign ring – a trace of that forbidden Fancy; there is something short and sharp in Bitzer, and the name seems to mix 'bitter' and 'bizarre'. Sleary suggests 'beery' and the slurred language of the half-drunk; there is a curtness about Sparsit, and it accords with sparseness of charity; Blackpool (Dickens thought first of John Prodge, then Stephen, George, old Stephen) and then plumped for the obviously northern name from the well-known Lancashire resort some twenty miles west of Preston; and James Harthouse (first drafted in Dickens's notes as Percy Harthouse, then renamed Jem and finally James) is indeed aptly and cynically named: he has no heart at all. *Hard Times*, though written in just over five months in the oppression of the demands of a weekly serial, reveals no consequent loss and even indicates a growing maturity in Dickens's skill in naming and depicting character.

Mr Gradgrind

'What I want is Facts.'

Mr Gradgrind, the retired wholesale hardware merchant, who boasts of being an eminently practical man, opens the entire story with a clear statement of his basic philosophy. His god is 'laissez-faire': a hard-headed sincere man, he is ruled by facts, cold and statistical, and is without sentiment (or so he believes). His name is meant to indicate his personality: to him everything can be graded and graduated, and fact-grinding is paramount. He rears his five children accordingly, and has married and treats his wife accordingly. His house, Stone Lodge, is his inanimate counterpart: practical, efficient, quite lacking in grace and imagination. The influence of his character and discipline are such that his son develops into a selfish hypocrite, his eldest daughter is frustrated and repressed, and only at her death does his wife come to realise that something has been missing – that which gives life its meaning – imagination and disinterested thought for others. The following references should be read and re-read, for the words of the author cannot be bettered in their scathing condemnation and derision of Gradgrind and his philosophy, I. i–iv; I. viii; I. xiv–xvi; II. xi–xii. Yet, and here he is totally unlike Mr Bounderby, he develops and changes. He has a better side, and is, despite himself, vulnerable to the stress of events. He is certainly doctrinaire and dogmatic, but what he does and says is sincere and not hypocritical. He is wrong, but sincerely wrong. He is fundamentally a worthy man, according to his lights. Within his limits he is an affectionate parent; he is apprehensive but aware of things outside his philosophy, and can show comparative kindness, and takes Sissy to his home to be educated and looked after. He realises and appreciates her value, despite her limitations according to his formidable criteria (I. xiv). He is affectionate towards Louisa, who disturbs him by their discussion over Bounderby's marriage proposals: he is not quite impervious, and takes refuge in statistics. Her return, distraught and near-disgraced, reveals to him, suddenly, sharply and thoroughly how wrong he has been, and he makes quick and tender recompense, although his world has been dashed about him. He is even strong enough in his new-dawning convictions to confess to Bounderby that perhaps, after all, they may have been wrong, and he stands up in a new contrasting light to that pompous and stubborn, infallible windbag. Even in the last indignity, where he, once the advocate of stark fact, has to connive at the felony of permitting his disgraced son to flee justice, the son who is not only a thief but a hypocrite and egoist too, he does not revert to his old hardness: not even when the model Bitzer, the crowning example of 'the system', throws that discipline tauntingly back to his face in a desperate moment. The bitterness, and the irony, is complete with Sleary's words 'It theemth to prethent . . . wayth of the dog ith!'. It is further noteworthy as a masterpiece of irony to witness how the Gradgrind who opens the story with such force is whittled down from a philosopher of Hard Facts into the symbol of

Hard Times, for ultimately, it is he and those derived from him who bear the brunt of all the tragedy, suffering and wrongdoing of the story.

Mr Bounderby

The Bully of humility.

Mr Bounderby is more than a symbol of the allegedly typical 'laissez-faire' magnate: he is drawn harshly, bitterly, even farcically and in caricature as a pompous, selfish, bigoted and cruel man. Unlike Mr Gradgrind, who is sincerely disinterested, though still wrong-minded, he is unaffected and essentially unabashed by having his system and past life exposed, and his 'Hard Fact' world proved false and unreal. Examples of his obvious pomposity and egoism can be found whenever he speaks: but others of his undesirable qualities need equal attention. He is sadistically cruel, and not merely in his most unsuitable marriage contract. Louisa has money, of course, and is considered a living testimonial to 'the system', both of which would attract Bounderby; yet note his callous treatment of his wife, whom he humiliates by his coarseness, brashness and deliberate avoidance of conventional politeness. Yet the sadistic streak of his nature emerges strongly in his treatment of Mrs Sparsit, actions of sheer spite against her veneer of high breeding. Only a bully and a coward would want to 'have the skin off her nose' and administer 'potent restoratives' such as screwing her thumbs and putting salt in her mouth, and, again in chagrin and spite, dismissing her so rudely. Sissy Jupe, as one of the strollers' children, must be sent packing on his famous 'Do it once' theory, and it is he who so curtly and cruelly tells her of her father's flight. Stephen Blackpool's bond of marriage is one 'for better for worse', but his own is peremptorily terminated on the grounds that 'the two horses wouldn't pull together', and thus is Louisa dismissed decisively and irrevocably with but five minutes' grace. Stephen Blackpool he hounds, virtually to death. His workpeople are 'Hands', and any of their aspirations are suspected and distorted: they are seeking 'turtle soup, and venison, and gold spoon' lives. He attracts only those elements – Tom, Bitzer, Mrs Sparsit, Harthouse – who respect and seek to maintain their safety within 'the system', regardless of the hypocrisy and shame involved in their servility to his position of power and his apparent achievement. He gloats over the errors and downfall of others (see particularly the Nickits episode, text, II. vii): he exudes hypocrisy, delighting in his self-made triumph and worshipping 'number one'. But all this is an enormous lie, based on a lie and hedged about by lies. Note the references to ditches and pigsties on his birthday, to the desertion of his mother and his abandonment to a drunken grandmother, to his bruises and punishments, to his sleeping on paving-stones as a ragged London street-boy, and a bit of riff-raff, cleaning boots, starved, poor and shoeless. All these, and many more not detailed here are calculated lies, exposed (in a brilliantly-constructed and devised scene) by his mother, the old woman Mrs Pegler (III. v) who has been pensioned off to keep her distance. His very name – how aptly and satirically chosen! – is a lie; yet see how he gloats when he hears that Stephen Blackpool has been forced to change his name in order to find work. The whole paragraph (III. iv) is a masterpiece of irony, and emphasises Bounderby's own discreditable nature. His blustering humility and total lack of imagination remain, even to the last: the chance he might have had, through the servile Bitzer, of crowing over Tom's felony is thwarted, and his spiteful reaction upon Mrs Sparsit produces her final outburst, appropriately and decisively, the last word on his windy and blustering character and temperament. He lives out his life, unchanged as at the beginning, in vanity and pretended humility, and is to leave behind him a legacy of bitterness and hatred, typically enough. He epitomises Dickens's hatred of the bullying profiteer type, risen from the ranks, graceless, heartless; an oppressor, greedy and callous, a Victorian 'rugged individual-ist', whose creed is summarised succinctly and ironically in Book I, Chapter V ('The M'Choakumchild school . . . without end, Amen.').

Louisa Gradgrind

'I have never had a child's belief or a child's fear.'

Louisa is the sacrifice on the altar of the Gradgrind–Bounderby philosophy: she it is who bears the brunt of the hard times, from childhood to virtual widowhood. Although other characters suffer in different measure (Blackpool, Sissy, Rachael, for example) Louisa throughout is oppressed by the system, and not only oppressed, but thwarted, stunted in imaginative growth, and thus made unsure of herself and of the basic principles of human contact and conduct. She is beset and bedevilled by an unimaginative but well-meaning father, a colourless mother, a selfish and hypocritical brother who uses her and her feelings for his own ends, and is matched, against her will, to a callous, bigoted and pompous husband. Small wonder, then, that she is easy prey – up to a point – for the idler and trifler Harthouse. The essential tragedy is that she does know of the world outside the Hard Fact school, symbolised by Sleary's circus and the bursting fire of the Coketown works (Book I. xv): she is blessed (or cursed in that society) with imagination and flights of fancy; she sees things in the embers. All this is burdened by the '-ologies' and other pressures, and is consequently limited and stunted, without bedrock of experience. Her natural instincts, of repulsion to Bounderby, for example (e.g. I. iv), are overlaid by her utilitarian environment. She is indeed, though not expressly, one of the 'innocents' murdered by the system: she has traces of self-will, and restless curiosity about that forbidden world of fancy, imagination and youthful enterprise (see I. iii; I. viii; I. ix). Sissy's different background is of intense interest to her, especially as it contains love and real family affection. Bounderby she has to tolerate despite herself, and marries him without a trace of affection or sentiment, quite unable to pierce his egotism or to make herself understood to her misguided father. Some crucial extracts need to be read and re-read as a revelation of her character and feelings: I. xiv; I. xv; II. xii. They show, more than detailed analysis and comment, that she is alive, with latent and untapped springs of emotion and love, yearning for understanding and sympathy. She receives none: her only outlet is her love for Tom, and this he soundly abuses and exploits. She is made desperate: 'What does it matter?' I. xv, and repeated II. ix. Her feelings are thus readily moved by a schemer, who uses Tom's affection for her as a lever. She is denied guidance, and is reduced to shame or flight: it is no triumph of the system that she instinctively choose the latter, and returns broken and distraught to her father's house, another proof of the system in all its inadequacies and anomalies. But the gospel of fact and hard-headed practical materialism cannot prevent imaginative thought: Louisa's natural and instinctive feelings, though forced inwards and mostly suppressed, lead her home, change Gradgrind's opinions, bring her to Sissy's side, and, at the last, are openly expressed in a future of some love and tenderness. Her story is another of Dickens's withering attacks upon a bleak philosophy of life and its human dangers; and a plea, through intense irony and drama, for true Christian charity, imagination and the education of the heart.

Thomas Gradgrind

The Whelp.

'The Whelp' is a convincing testimony to the inadequacies and false values of 'the system'. It is perhaps impossible to separate utterly Nature from nurture, but Tom's childhood background (I. iii) counts for a great deal. Led by his more self-willed sister, he remains a passive culprit before his outraged father (I. iii): he is sulky, sullen and obviously suppressed at home, recognising the bases of his moods and limitations (I. viii). He lacks imagination, the hall-mark of progress in the Gradgrind method, but he knows how to play on his sister's limited affections, and how to use her to manage Bounderby: this is the thin end of the wedge, so to speak, and the beginnings of his pivotal role in the plot. Thus it is that he encourages Louisa, for his own selfish ends, to encounter Bounderby (I. ix), and when he eventually goes to Bounderby's bank, the system that promotes 'number one' and encourages 'rugged individualism' (see beginning of I. xiv) finds him an apt disciple: Louisa's marriage is helpful to him as a personal lever, and delights him alone, for it is quite clear that Louisa's emotions (except of dislike and resentment) are not involved. So cushioned and protected, knowing that Louisa will always support him, he rapidly degenerates. He grows indolent and indifferent so far as his work is concerned: his attitude to Bounderby is objectionable (for he is, after all, his employer); he runs up gambling debts, putting on ill-fitting airs, knowing that Louisa will always rescue him from the worst consequences. Most reprehensible of all, he openly boasts of all these things to a comparative stranger, Harthouse, and succeds only in proving his hypocrisy and selfishness (II. iii). He is, regrettably, the only object of Louisa's real affections, having enjoyed a close childhood, perhaps driven together under 'the system' for mutual solace in their dreadful house of '-ologies'. But he uses and abuses her love and trust abominably, gloating over it, exploiting it, with the odd pang of conscience indeed, but yet so instilled with the precepts of the self-centred system and its 'number one' philosophy that he can involve the harmless and trusting Blackpool, quite deliberately and in all malice, with his plan to free himself of debt by robbing the bank. In this sense, indeed, he is responsible for Blackpool's death. His later days are hounded and uncomfortable, clouded in deceit and weak remorse. The dying Stephen incriminates him (III. vi), and only Sissy's quick thinking saves him from immediate exposure. How bitterly ironic are his last days in England! The wheel turns full circle for him too. The boy who peeped curiously into Sleary's circus is now the man who, in all humiliation and disgrace, has to be disguised as a member of Sleary's troupe to avoid arrest, and has to escape from Bitzer through Sleary's intervention and his intelligent circus animals! Another model product of the system dies belatedly penitent, indeed, and there is little good to be said of him until then. He spoils, injures and wounds everyone involved with him. Like Bitzer, he is at once a representative and a condemnation of Victorian utilitarianism, and the bitter satire of his final conversation with his father (especially III. vii; 'I don't see why. . . . Comfort yourself!') completes Dickens's indictment of a heartless and inhumane social system.

Cecilia (Sissy) Jupe

'An affectionate, earnest, good young woman.'

Like all those not affected by or not understanding 'the system', Sissy has the natural instincts and feelings of compassion, sympathy and imagination. She is alive, sensitive, generous, not in spite of but because of her origins and early warm family life. Her introduction in the second chapter needs to be carefully noted: it opens the bitter, wry, sardonic tone of the novel, and presents her opposed to the calculations and pretensions of the Gradgrind–Bounderby philosophy. Materially her life has not been so comfortable: she is but a circus-clown's child: but she it is who, compared with the colourless Bitzer, has all the warmth and deep emotion. She has been able to enjoy what we would consider a normal happy childhood: her father has done all he could for her, and when he himself knows that he is failing in his work he takes the agonising step of abandoning her, so that she may improve herself unhampered by his burdens (I. vi; I. ix). Taken in hand so brusquely by the systematic Gradgrind, Bounderby and the aptly-named M'Choakumchilds, she is bewildered and quite out of her depth and sentiments, yet her natural instincts are right. She sees through the coldness of statistical fact. Louisa soon admits Sissy's better relationship with Mrs Gradgrind, and she retains that saving grace of free imagination, unstultified by the battering and the hardness of Fact (e.g. Book I, end of Chapter II; Chapter IX, beginning of Chapter XIV). How farcical it is that she, born and bred in the circus, cannot define a horse (according to Gradgrind): yet this 'girl number twenty' has a sweetening influence on the whole Gradgrind household. She is a solace to the desperate Louisa, and shrewdly intelligent as to Tom's delinquency. Her association with Rachael (e.g. III. v) is born of sympathy and compassion, and leads directly to the discovery of Stephen's fate. She it is who summons help: she it is who saves Tom – not worth saving – through those old companions of hers she was once asked to forswear and forget. She rebuffs Harthouse, and shames that indolent and sensual man into prompt scurrying away from the scene of his misdemeanours. Although her father has died by the end of the novel, her experiences, faith and trust, as seen by Mr Sleary (III. viii), give the lie to the Gradgrind philosophy and her future is one, almost the only one, of contentment and fulfilment.

Sissy, of course, is symbolic: the strength of the novel in that she represents that loving trustful humanity which Dickens felt was the basic fundamental need of the times, in all relationships. She is a symbol of an influence which changes people's thoughts and attitudes: and thus she performs, among other things, that vital function of demonstrating the difference between the wrong, but sincerely wrong Gradgrind and the pompous windbag Bounderby, who is fixed and unchangeable in his egotism and hypocrisy. She grows, she develops, and in fact takes on the whole final movements which lead to the climax and 'solution' of the novel in her dealings with Louisa, Rachael, Harthouse, and Tom. She is essentially disinterested, unselfish, thinking and caring only for others; and with her Dickens has created, in a masterly study, an entirely convincing and psychologically sound picture.

Bitzer

The colourless boy.

All the characters in *Hard Times* are threaded relevantly and strongly into the fabric of the story, acting and reacting with others in a complete plot. Bitzer is no exception. He represents a complete and completed study of the model of perfectibility, according to the criteria and code of the Gradgrind–Bounderby philosophy. He remains unchanged throughout the movement of the story: colourless, unmoved by feelings of sympathy or compassion, completely unimaginative, yet shrewdly aware of 'number one', and obsequious to a degree. He is well described (in Chapter II); his real nature appears early (I. v), and he is soon in servile attendance on Bounderby as his light porter at the bank (I. i). He is clearly and brutally described in his development and fixed attitudes: a carrier of tales, humourless, without passion, even without filial affection, looking down upon the workpeople of Coketown with disdain and condescension. He talks to Blackpool, for example, curtly and brusquely. He is nonplussed by the robbery – after all, he was sleeping on the premises and carried responsibility with Mrs Sparsit for its security – but he knows exactly the contents of Tom's safe, and has early suspicions. He accompanies Louisa to her dying mother, '. . . fit colourless servitor at Death's door,' and does not reappear until the closing stages of the story, now as the methodical systematic observer of Tom's (and everyone's) behaviour, knowing that he will rise further in Bounderby's esteem by the apprehension of the culprit, possibly assuming Tom's position in the bank. The Gradgrind philosophy is dissected and found perfect (III. viii): although he is in fact deprived of his conquest, we know of his future, maintained by his master in the Bounderby mould. He is the real success of the system, and its strongest condemnation.

Stephen Blackpool

A man of perfect integrity.

Blackpool's story is simply and clearly told against the Coketown background (beginning of I. v, x–xiii; II. iv–vi; and III. iv–vi). He and his lot in life are graphically and sympathetically described: the honest uneducated but not unintelligent workman, harassed by external troublemakers, expecting but little help and advice from his employer yet receiving more kicks than credit. His fellow-workers are incited against him, his employer has neither the imagination nor the inclination to understand his difficulties, and his marriage has turned sour. Throughout, however, though oppressed and tormented, he is equable, quiet, passive (perhaps too much so) and endlessly perplexed by the complications of existence. Rachael it is who brings out the best in him, emphasising his integrity, essential honesty and tenderness. He is, perhaps, drawn too perfectly and idealistically, too much a symbol of Dickens's indignant sympathy for the injustices under which many workers suffered. Yet he has an understandable moment of weakness (I. xiii): otherwise he shows courage and endurance in the torture of his wretched wife's degradation and interference; he stands up to Bounderby and Slackbridge, accepts his ostracism, and leaves resolutely all he has known and understood in the hope of better things. Endlessly perplexed and puzzled, he cannot understand why, having done no harm himself, he should be so troubled and exploited. The economic machinery is too much for him, and it is to him that Dickens gives a bitter denunciation of 'laissez-faire' principles and of the antagonisms they produce (II. v; III. vi). He it is who falls into the pit, literally and symbolically. His terrible death, poignant and exonerating, seems inevitable and yet fulfilling: he finds his peace, through pain and struggle, and is comforted at the last by the presence of the woman he loves. He shames the rest by his genuine humility, his lack of artifice, and by his kindliness and integrity.

It should, however, be mentioned that Blackpool, taken out of the novel, so to speak, as Dickens's only industrial worker, and symbolising as a consequence much that Dickens thought of the 'working-classes', is not entirely successfully drawn. The accent in which he speaks is mixed – a minor point. But the background of Stephen's story is untrue (see 'Background' pp. 16–19), and it is difficult to understand why a worker would not associate with his Union's decision to better conditions (although Slackbridge is not meant to be an engaging personality) simply because he has promised a trusted woman friend that he will stay clear of trouble. He cannot be considered typical of the working classes of that age or of any other. But he plays out Dickens's intention to expose a sufferer in the hard winter of materialism, in all his isolation. He is a new kind of man in Dickens's fantastic gallery of people, an earnest sober industrial worker, contributing his share to the world's wealth, yet sharing little of it himself in a society whose workings he is not meant to understand.

Mrs Sparsit

A highly connected lady.

Mrs Sparsit, a veritable bird of prey, is called by Tom, irreverently but pertinently, 'Mother Sparsit': she is almost grotesque, with her Roman nose and black eyebrows dominating the various establishments into which she firmly settles herself. Introduced in all her glory and self-esteem (Book I. vii), her pretensions stripped bare by Dickens right from the start, she shows up as a servile flatterer, enjoying a melodramatic and genteel pride over her rather unremarkable past and present status. She is helped in her assumed independence and detachment by Bounderby's deliberate use of her as a foil to his own pretensions of a lowly and despicable (and of course thus entirely fabricated) early history. Bounderby gloats over her downfall in society, though of course she has never been that exalted, as it enhances his own self-promotion. But Mrs Sparsit is no fool. She is not slow to use her position, making the negative slights of her employer into a positive virtue for her own security. As the popular saying goes, she knows 'which side her bread is buttered'. She can be pertinently shrewd, and she can manage Bounderby in his blustering moods. She installs herself in the bank quarters, the 'Bank Dragon' to the Coketowners, and there gossips, intrigues and exchanges confidences, up to a certain point, with the equally obsequious Bitzer: she sees through Harthouse's schemes readily enough. Up to his marriage she reveres and respects Bounderby: but she has no time for Louisa, of course, who has altered the routine of her life somewhat. She never loses an opportunity of slighting her, or of reminding Bounderby of the 'good old days' they enjoyed in his bachelorhood, comfortably alone. After the robbery, from the shock of which she has to recover at Bounderby's country seat, she uses her influence to the full to damage Louisa's relationship (not that it needs much aggravation) with Bounderby. Above all, in her prowling ubiquity, thrusting her Roman nose thoroughly into everyone's affais, she sees in Harthouse's contact with Louisa (closer through her provocation of the testy and uncouth Bounderby) her great chance to reveal herself as Bounderby's truest and most devoted servant. The whole account (II. x–xi; III. iii), and that of her next escapade, the 'discovery' of Mrs Pegler with its disastrous dénouement, is told with typical Dickensian gusto and with a wry, sardonic humour. All her affectations and artificial gentility, all her jealousy of and contempt for Louisa, all her servility and cunning are eventually frustrated and deflated into almost comic hopelessness. Her efforts lead directly to her dismissal and punishment by the callous Bounderby, to whom human beings are dispensable (III. ix), though she speaks her mind, truthfully, at the last. Her future is to be distinctly unpleasant, but such is a fitting end to false pride, artifice, obsequiousness and lack of charity. Dickens hated privilege and systems of patronage: he despised snobbishness and self-righteousness and bigotry. In his portrait of the life and eventual distress of Mrs Sparsit he sums up much of these feelings with that telling caricature and burlesque which make the truth so sharp and painful.

Minor characters

In one sense, there are no minor characters in *Hard Times*: there are so few characters altogether that each plays a distinctive and important part in the plot and in the fulfilment of Dickens's purpose, and all are tightly interwoven into the fabric of the story. Nevertheless, some play an external part: that is to say, they act and react on other characters, or play some role (perhaps none the less important) on the outside of the main theme. In some cases they are deliberately played down by Dickens so as to give special eminence and authority to others, especially to Gradgrind and Bounderby. Thus they need to be noted with care.

Mrs Gradgrind, 'A little, thin, white, pink-eyed bundle of shawls, of surpassing feebleness', is dominated by her husband and his theories: she is an ineffectual mother (rather like Mrs Matthew Pocket in *Great Expectations*), and serves to emphasise Gradgrind's supreme authority. Lifeless, colourless, pushed into the background, she has yet a supreme moment in the story in her death (at the end of II. ix). Only at the last, through Sissy's influence in her household, does she realise that something has been missing, something vital and crucial in life. In passages of supreme drama and pathos (one critic has called it 'imaginative genius') Dickens portrays her last moments and thoughts, in her attempt to write down that 'something – not an Ology at all' was omitted in the system.

The political agent James Harthouse deserves notice as pushing on the plot towards Gradgrind's belated conversion, and for revealing much of Louisa's nature. His cultivated languor, his 'accession of boredom' (reminding one of Wrayburn in *Our Mutual Friend*) is no pose: he symbolises that parasitism in society which Dickens loathed. Coketown soon bores him, but he employs his time in attempting to seduce Louisa. Like the hypocrite Bounderby, he uses 'the system' for his own ends, and is eventually disposed of by Sissy, appropriately enough.

Sleary, proprietor of the travelling circus, deserves attention, for he and his troupe symbolise the 'other side of the hill', the world of art and fancy, deplored, derided and condemned by the 'Hard Fact' men. With his preposterous accent, 'never sober and never drunk', he and his troupe (see especially I. vi; III. vii) open and close the movement of the story, and have a philosophy of 'Fancy' which overrides and overrules that of Fact.

Rachael, kindly, patient, tolerant, plays a useful part throughout the novel as a centre of affection and guidance: another whose 'heart' is in the right place, and who suffers from the Coketown world of fact. This 'sweet-tempered and serene' working-woman (whose accent, oddly enough, is not stressed as in dialect, which is surely strange) links Blackpool and his wretched wife, Louisa and Sissy, and plays a significant part in the tense delay, and then the discovery of Stephen.

Mrs Pegler, 'that maligned old lady', early suspected as a close link with Bounderby, provides some of the most comic yet most ironical passages in the book. Pensioned off and kept at a distance by her son, she is dragged into the light by the indefatigable Mrs Sparsit, only to reveal herself as Bounderby's mother, and not as an accessory to the robbery. In an extraordinary scene (III. v) she accomplishes, unwittingly, Bounderby's deflation, for which one has long waited.

Structure

The construction of *Hard Times*, like its plot, is simple and
direct: it is chronological, economic and stark. After one reading, a glance down the 'Contents' page is sufficient to recapi-
tulate the movement and connections of the story (although,
of course, further, more detailed readings are needed for a
thorough understanding of the text itself). In his manuscript
Dickens divided the book (remember that it was to appear
first as a weekly serial) into five monthly parts, a system to
which he was long familiar: he then arranged his material
into weekly issues. It was by these larger monthly units, not
apparent in the serial or in the book as now printed, that he
measured his progress and calculated the ground still to be
covered. The opening words of Book I. viii mark the beginning of the second monthly division, and indicate that the
background and general exposition have been completed:
the second division ended with Louisa's marriage to Bounderby (I. xvi); the third with Stephen Blackpool's turning his
back on Coketown (II. vi); the fourth ended with the breakdown of Louisa's marriage (III. iii), and the fifth, of course, is
completed with the ending of the entire story. Each of these is
a well-marked and important stage of the novel's development.

Dickens also directed his readers' attention to the movement and structure of his story by those larger trends which
comprised the three 'Books': Sowing, Reaping, Garnering.
This was an old device, dating back in English novel literature
from Fielding's *Joseph Andrews* (1742), but Dickens had not
used it before – except in the serial form, but not the volume
edition, of *Oliver Twist*. Although it was apparently too late to
use this device in the serialised version it is known that Dickens had decided from the first on these named divisions, which
were printed in when the novel was reissued in volume form,

the sections coinciding with what had been the end of the second and fourth monthly 'parts'.

No elaborately detailed examination of structure is demanded for such a short compact novel: but several consecutive points are worth careful recognition. Note how the arch-priest of Fact, Gradgrind, begins and dominates the opening of the story: he represents the theory that Dickens is setting out to deride and demolish, and thus Gradgrind opens the whole plot, in his own school, in which Bitzer and Sissy Jupe, the rising generation to be bred on Fact, are tersely introduced. By Chapter III we know of Gradgrind's family; and by the end of the chapter (the end of the first weekly number) Bounderby is mentioned, later developed against the colourless background of Mrs Gradgrind (Chapter IV). The murky atmosphere of Coketown, and its influence, are then drawn in as the two local magnates and 'Hard Fact' men walk through its streets, not knowing the poorer end of their own town (Chapter V), and more is learnt of Sissy Jupe, her family and associations (Chapter VI). Then Mrs Sparsit, the complement to Mr Bounderby, is drawn into the story (Chapter VIII) with her employer, making a remarkable and skilful, and grossly ironic, picture of false gentility and false humility. Already one feels suspicious and anxious, wondering what 'Fancy' is obtruding and dominant where 'Fact' is so cultivated and exalted. One must note the description of the circus-folk and their leader, Mr Sleary (I. vi), with their gentility, lack of affectation or self-deception, their compassion and respectability, with a kindly philosophy of Fancy opposed to Gradgrind and Bounderby's philosophy of Fact: Sissy Jupe's transfer from one environment to another is significant and symbolic.

The novel progresses with more detail of Tom's relations with his sister (Chapter VIII), Sissy's development (Chapter IX), and then the entry of the industrial aspect of Coketown with Blackpool's (and Rachael's) story of his marital perplexities (Chapters X–XIII), linking these with the old woman (Mrs Pegler), another significant strand later to be drawn together into the fabric of the story with devastating effect. Then 'Time went on': the chronology develops (Chapter XIV), the youngsters have grown up and Louisa marries Bounderby. It must be mentioned here that Dickens had foreseen the necessity of introducing Harthouse quite early: as he noted, 'The man who, being utterly sensual, and careless, comes to very much the same thing in the end as the Grindgrind school? Not yet.' He delayed his appearance until it was more effective, and the Second Book, Reaping, introduces him (I. i) into the Sparsit–Bitzer clique, then to the 'Hard Fact' men, and finally to his eventual quarry, Louisa Bounderby. The tragic story of his heartless involvement with Louisa, under Mrs Sparsit's close vigilance, takes up the story across that of Blackpool's resistance to the Union and Bounderby, leading to his dismissal (Chapters IV–VI): Harthouse gains Louisa's untutored confidence, almost destroying her integrity (Chapter VII). The bank robbery is skilfully interwoven here as an interlude. Bounderby's retreat into the country (II. vii) spaces out the characters, and heightens their movement, and the push of the story towards Louisa's seemingly-inevitable disgrace grows in pace and tension (Chapters VIII–IX), held up temporarily by Mrs Gradgrind's death.

Again the theme is re-established, as Harthouse's pursuit of Louisa continues (Chapters X–XI), exploding into the unexpected return of Louisa to her father's house, closing the Second Book. The Third winds up the bitter story. Gradgrind knows he has been in error; he at least is redeemable. Gradgrind returns to the centre of things, seeing that his education of Louisa and Tom has failed, miserably and wretchedly. Then Sissy's effect upon his household (and himself) is made clear. Sissy too rebuffs Harthouse (Chapter II), an episode in essence like a fairy tale (compare 'Jack the Giant-killer'). Bounderby

is unchanged and unchangeable, despite Gradgrind's ex-
planations and his wife's departure: and the suspense over
Blackpool is excellently maintained until his discovery, bridging Mrs Pegler's astounding revelations (Chapter V) in a
lurid and pathetic scene (Chapter VI). The wheel turns full
circle. Gradgrind has yet to face further humiliation over his
reprobate son (Chapters VII–VIII), and we find ourselves
back with the circus-folk again in all their warmth, family
solidity and helpfulness. The final chapter is an epilogue,
but the real last words of the story are Mr Sleary's on his
philosophy of life, the philosophy of Fancy:

'. . . One, that there ith a love in the world, not all Thelf-interetht
after all, but something very different; t'other, that it hath a way of
ith own of calculating or not calculating, whith thomehow or another
ith at leatht ath hard to give a name to, ath the wayth of dogth ith!'
(III. viii).
    'People muth be amuthed. They can't be alwayth a learning, nor
yet they can't be alwayth a working, they an't made for it. You *mutht*
have uth, Thquire. Do the withe thing and the kind thing too, and
make the betht of uth; not the wurtht!' (III. viii).

A further and final note on internal structure must be noticed;
it is the skill with which Dickens, in a short and compressed
novel, includes and inter-crosses so many human relationships, each of which deserve close attention and study, sep-
arately and in comparison. There are husbands and wives,
such as Mr and Mrs Gradgrind, Mr and Louisa Bounderby,
Mr and Mrs Jupe and the ill-matched Blackpools. There are,
of course, the important parent–children relationships,
not forgetting Sissy's own children, and brothers and sisters;
and one must not forget Mr Bounderby's treatment of his
mother, nor Bitzer's treatment of his. Note too Louisa's
emotions at her mother's death. Various masters and servants, or other dependants, are treated: and the action and
reaction of others such as Rachael, Sleary, Slackbridge and
Harthouse, as external contacts are important. So are the
implications of the influence of the M'Choakumchilds and the

Government officer on children, and of Lady Scadgers on Mrs Sparsit.

This is a narrow canvas for Dickens, but the interrelationships and influences are all made clear, often brutally clear, and in them we have a whole society in movement and agitation, and human nature displayed in its remarkable variety.

Style

The eighteenth-century French naturalist Buffon, in one of his remarkable generalisations, said that 'Le style c'est l'homme' – 'The style is the man himself'. With no one is this truer than with Dickens, generally throughout his two dozen or so novels, and particularly with *Hard Times*. Here he was angry and bitter: he always wrote with gusto and vigour, with tremendous vitality and scope; he always expressed sympathy and indignation with suffering; his narrative technique and descriptive abilities were cultivated and vividly effective; and he was not afraid of displaying emotion and sentiment, even in excess. Above all, he strove for simplicity and directness. He learned early that great factor in all good writing – to have something to say, and to say it.

But *Hard Times* is unique among his writings for its economy and conciseness, induced, as has frequently been mentioned, by the nature of its weekly serial publication. No other of Dickens's works is so restricted, so stark, so dramatic or allegorical in form. Dickens had to express his meaning and purpose tersely and sharply; he had to pack in not so much lengthy description and incidental character (as in one of his usual enormous canvases) but to pierce through the underlying *meaning* of the society and people with whom he was concerned. Minute detail, therefore, of character and place, he dispensed with. It was replaced by what can only be called a new aspect of Dickens's skill, a compression and a swiftness, an ability to describe and set an atmosphere in a few vivid strokes, that he had never before used and was never again to attempt.

The matter is best studied by examples. Take, for instance, the description of Coketown: 'It was a town of red brick . . . the last and the next' (Book I. v); 'In the hardest working part of Coketown . . . forty years of age' (I. x); 'A sunny midsummer day . . . looks upon to bless' (opening, Book II); or the description of Gradgrind (I. i), Bounderby (I. iv), and of Harthouse (II. i). This is not mere description, though that is skilfully accomplished: it is also comment, significant emotional and intellectual comment, packed with symbol and meaning. Within each, by careful reading and re-reading, one begins to see the 'art which conceals art' of Dickens's extraordinary style. The first-mentioned piece may serve as an illustration (which the student is recommended to try for himself throughout similar passages).

It should be noted that despite the tight construction and economical writing of the book, scenic and other 'background' description is not only symbolic and suggestive, and sympathetic (that is, corresponding and contributing to the mood and atmosphere), but also exposes a full range of sensations. Many authors, not necessarily inferior or superficial in their style or content, are satisfied with a purely visual effect. The visual impact of Dickens is always strong, but other senses are provoked, equally sharply and penetratingly, in *Hard Times*, which is nevertheless a narrative satire in principle and not in any sense a tale dependent on purely descriptive passages, apart from those presenting human character. Sound, for example, is not neglected, as in Gradgrind's dry cracking voice in the first two chapters, the noise of Sleary's Horse-riding in Chapter III (and Sleary's own 'pursy' pronunciation throughout), Bounderby's metallic laugh and 'brassy speaking-trumpet of a voice' in Chapter IV, and the noises of Coketown (V, paragraph 2): all these are examples from the early pages, easily supplemented from the rest of the book.

Many authors avoid descriptions or even mention of smell, possibly because these may be in themselves unpleasant and also because there is a limited vocabulary available for their description. Dickens, however, comments appropriately on the 'drainage and water-services' and the 'damp mortar' of Stone Lodge, on the 'ill-smelling dye' of Coketown's river, and the general airlessness of the 'hardest working part of

Coketown' (Chapter X, paragraph 2). Later on (II. i) the town 'seems to be frying in oil', Bounderby praises its general smokiness (II. ii) and the ill-smelling river is again mentioned (II. iii). At II. viii ('Explosion') the scents of Harthouse's tobacco and of the summer air combine to produce the 'sympathetic' background to the idler's self-satisfaction and complacency. Escape from the smoky atmosphere of Coketown provides the reason for the stroll of Sissy and Rachael into the countryside (III. vi) with all its consequences. It is, however, curious that the inevitable smells of the circus are not mentioned.

Other kinds of impression (e.g. touch) are also to be found: in his very choice of vocabulary and phraseology, in using such devises as alliteration, assonance, onomatopoeia and climax, Dickens conveys by sense and sound (neither at the expense of the other) the impact he wishes to achieve. The symbolic impressions of Coketown have already been noted: the student would do well to read and then re-read the following extracts, paying the closest attention to both construction and style, down to the very words themselves. Such analysis reveals the tremendous force and skill of Dickens's writing, and his full range of appeal to mind and ear. The list does not pretend to be exhaustive, of course, and merely indicates the various types of writing which deserve attention. I. i, paragraph 2; I. ii, 'The square finger . . . bleed white'; I. ii, the penultimate (i.e. last but one) paragraph; I. iii, paragraphs 4–7; I. iv, 'He was a rich man . . . humility' – this is a good illustration of what is technically called anaphora; the descriptions of Coketown in I. v and x, and II. i; the last paragraph of I. xii – anaphora again; the sympathetic background of I. xiii, 'The wind was blowing . . . repeated' and 'the wind blew . . . life'; the last four paragraphs of II. ix; II. xi – the whole chapter 'Lower and Lower' is brilliantly written, especially the details of Mrs Sparsit's stealthy pursuit 'in the thick dust that felt like velvet', with the sympathetic background of the storm; and III. vi, especially the beginning and the end.

Note again (I. v). Dickens, as he says, is striking 'a key-note': this is our introduction to the restricted setting of the whole novel, and it is crucially important that the fullest impact is made. The name itself is significant. The first sentence begins with a normal description, and then qualifies it, to establish the precise desired effect, terminating with a vivid simile. The very impersonal pronoun 'It' introduces each of the four sentences, with deliberate repetition. Note the colours, the smell, the atmosphere of smoke and noise, the monotony – again accomplished by deliberate repetition, deliberate monotony of construction – and the pervading comment. There is no doubt what Dickens wants one to think of the place: he has set the scene, and given it its atmosphere.

In other places, too, the atmosphere is tautly suggested, always relevant and appropriate to events. Outstanding examples (there are many others) are those of the schoolroom at the very begininng, the figures of Sissy and Bitzer (in the second chapter), Stone Lodge (beginning Chapter III), the factory (I. xi), Gradgrind's study (Chapter XV), Louisa's retreat (II. vii) and return home (in II. ix). Note especially how the elements play their part in Mrs Sparsit's prowling pursuit of Louisa (II. xi), the storm erupting in phase with the movement of the story; note too the atmosphere of the scene in which Blackpool is found, beginning (III. vi) with the outskirts of Coketown, in fresh countryside, and ending, in a lurid torchlight scene, with the funeral stretcher of the mangled and asphyxiated Blackpool. In each instance, description is intermingled with comment: Dickens is not merely describing a place or a scene; he is ensuring that it is viewed coloured by the appropriate emotion.

A word need perhaps be said concerning Dickens's style in characterisation, for it is connected too with other aspects of his writing. It may seem, at first glance, that the characters are described or presented in such a way that they could not be real; they could not really be true or alive. Some seem grotesque, farcical, theatrical, or merely ridiculous. This point is connected with what is often called 'realism': but a clear distinction must be made. The term could mean, as it often does in painting, a reproduction of something so that it is instantly recognisable for what it is. It is a duplicate of the actual, in some other form or presentation. But Dickens's realism, particularly with his characters, is not of this type. They are founded on actuality; they are made up of what one can see and hear, talk to and exchange words and ideas with; they seem to look real, but he is making the impossible seem probable by sheer force, emphasis, and often deliberate exaggeration to the point of absurdity. Bounderby and Mrs Sparsit, for example, noted carefully and taken literally, seem grotesque: but they are nevertheless typical. In this connection the words of the American philosopher George Santayana may make the point clearer, but would deserve quotation otherwise.

When people say that Dickens exaggerates, it seems to me they can have no eyes and no ears. They probably have only *notions* of what things and people are; they accept them conventionally, at their diplomatic value. Their minds run on in the region of discourse, where there are masks only and no faces, ideas and no facts; they have little sense for those living grimaces that play from moment to moment upon the countenance of the world . . .! surely I never looked like that. Mere caricature, farce, and horse play. Dickens exaggerates. . .! But the polite world is lying; there *are* such people; we are such people ourselves in our true moments, in our veritable impulses; but we are careful to stifle and hide those moments from ourselves and from the world; to purse and pucker ourselves into the mask of our conventional personality; and so simpering, we profess that it is very coarse and inartistic of Dickens to undo our life's work for us in an instant, and remind us of what we are.*

Relevant to *Hard Times*, one may note those personal mannerisms underlining a character: Gradgrind's square finger, Bounderby's throwing on of his hat, Mrs Sparsit's movement of her Roman nose and black eyebrows, Louisa's gazing into the fire, and Bitzer's knuckling of his forehead, among others.

* George Santayana *Works*, Vol. II (1936).

There is too some compelling phrase or sentence about each character (often several) which deserves notice.

Dickens wrote with great strength and force, even under strain (and we know he found difficulty with the space-limitations of *Hard Times*). There is tremendous gusto and vitality in his descriptions of people, and in other parts of the novel too. The accounts of the 'Horse-riding', all Bounderby's hypocritical antics, poor Sissy's struggles, Slackbridge's demagogue-like harangues, Mrs Sparsit's pursuit of Louisa and Harthouse (II. xi and III. iii) and her next 'discovery' (III. v), all these, and others, are written with an intense exuberance and vitality.

The novel abounds in what may be called verbal felicity, a neat turn of phrase or sentence, making some point sharply and happily. There are so very many that only a few need be mentioned as examples: 'He had reached the neutral ground upon the outskirts of the town, which was neither town nor country, and yet was either spoiled.' 'A man who was the Bully of humility.' '. . . Under the influence of that wintry piece of fact, she would become torpid again.' 'He sat writing in the room with the deadly statistical clock, proving something no doubt – probably, in the main, that the Good Samaritan was a Bad Economist.' 'A great Pyramid of failure.' '. . . As if he ran himself into a white heat, when other people ran themselves into a glow.' 'Mrs Sparsit sat by the fire, with her foot in her cotton stirrup, little thinking whither she was posting.'

Two final aspects need be noted: pathos and humour. Dickens could verge on and indeed drop into sentimentality, even falling into poetical rhythms in his prose in moments of deep emotion. In *Hard Times*, never forgetting his underlying purpose, he does not seem to exceed the conventional bounds, but in his treatment of the desperate Louisa, in the death of Mrs Gradgrind, and in the scene of Stephen's discovery and eventual death, he has written prose (especially with the second mentioned) which defies analysis and criticism. With the surest touch, with perfect cadences and movement in his words and sentences, Dickens here shows his conscientious literary craftsmanship at its best. It is impossible, unless one is quite insensitive, not to be moved by these scenes. Their undertones are poetic, almost Biblical; they are full of symbolism and metaphor, of sympathy and understanding.

It is generally considered that Dickens is one of the world's great literary humorists: he was personally described by one of his friends as 'the cheerfullest man of his age', and we know of his high-spirited and irresistible vivacity in portraying such characters as Pickwick, Micawber, Wopsle, Traddles, Swiveller, and countless others. But there are no characters, except perhaps Childers and Kidderminster (I. vi), who are engaged in any direct humour in *Hard Times*. There are humorous incidents, of course, but there is no trace of comedy in the sense of 'being funny'. The comic element is based on satire, on a biting and ridiculing satire: pure comic invention as such would have been out of place in the novel in which Dickens was intent on striking what he called the heaviest blow in his power for the victims of industrial oppression. It is an indictment, aggressive and forceful, and the theme is pursued throughout with relentless and trenchant satire. Repeatedly, through the dialogue, in his own comments, as an essential backbone to the plot, and in countless words and gestures, Dickens satirises his characters, their situations and reactions. That is the whole tone and underlying emotion of the novel, and can be illustrated from any and every page: it is important to observe its presence and scope as one reads the text.

General questions and sample answer in note form

1 In what various ways (give specific examples) are 'Fact' and 'Fancy' illustrated and contrasted within the characters and incidents of *Hard Times*?

2 Summarise the plot of *Hard Times* (in about forty lines), showing how Dickens develops his themes.

3 Give a true account of the bank robbery: why was it committed, and what were its major consequences? Were they all foreseen by Tom?

4 What are the most vivid impressions which remain with you of Coketown? How does Dickens describe its atmosphere, industry and people?

5 What scenes in *Hard Times* are laid outside Coketown itself? Is there any added importance in their being set beyond the limits of Coketown's industrial atmosphere?

6 Bounderby is described as 'The Bully of humility'. Say what you think this means, giving examples of this attitude from different parts of the story.

7 What kind of home-life is enjoyed, or endured, by the Gradgrind family before and after Sissy Jupe's joining them?

8 Stephen Blackpool has been called a 'dramatic perfection, instead of a characteristic example of an honest workman'. Give your own estimate of his character, and describe one incident in which he plays a major part.

9 Discuss carefully the significance of Sleary and his circus troupe throughout the entire novel: what kind of man was Sleary himself?

10 Why was James Harthouse introduced into the plot: is his part vital? Show by reference to specific examples how different people estimate his character.

11 What have you found particularly interesting in the characters of Bitzer and Mrs Sparsit? Why do you think each is presented so that you cannot like them, but yet remain highly interested in their activities and views?

12 Briefly recount the part played by Rachael in the story, and show how it touches the lives of many other characters.

13 In your opinion, which are the most, and which the least, likeable characters of the book, and why? With whom do you feel the most sympathy?

14 Giving specific examples, show how coincidence plays an essential part in the plot. Is it ever stretched so far that it seems incredible or artificial?

15 What different family relationships are described and developed in the novel? Give an account of any two contrasting kinds.

16 'It is an analysis and a condemnation of the ethos of industrialism.' Show by three or four specific examples how the novel both analyses and condemns some of the 'laissez-faire' conditions of 19th-century industrial England.

17 Can you think of any reasons why *Hard Times* was for long regarded as one of Dickens's lesser, inferior novels?

18 Of this book Lord Macaulay said: 'One or two passages of exquisite pathos an the rest sullen Socialism.' Consider this criticism: pick out what you think are passages of pathos, and indicate by reference what you believe he is suggesting by 'sullen Socialism'.

19 What has impressed you most about Dickens's style of writing in *Hard Times*? Without attempting to quote at length, refer to some incidents or characters which seem to you to have been described with sharpness and economy, or with what is often called 'Dickensian gusto'.

20 A critic wrote of this novel that it is 'the least read of the novels and probably also the least enjoyed by those who read it'. Give reasons for your having enjoyed (or not enjoyed) the reading and perhaps re-reading of *Hard Times*.

21 Give a brief account of any novel you have read, or any play you have seen in the theatre or on TV which is set almost entirely in an industrial background, past or present.

22 From one or two books you have read or studied, describe the conequences, on the partners or their children, of the breakdown of a marriage.

23 Consider the 'pros and cons' of the news that 'Workers' strikes can never be justified, and should be forbidden by law'.

24 In your personal reading which do you prefer, Fact or Fiction? Give examples of, and your reasons for, your choice.

25 In your opinion should circuses continue to be considered suitable public entertainment? Try to weigh up likely opposing views.

26 Describe a character in a book you have read or studied who yields to temptation: indicate, briefly, the consequences.

27 Many writers have had alternative names for their novels and plays long before they have written out the entire work. Can you think of any alternative titles for any book, play or long poem you have read, and explain how – in any way you choose – they could be appropriate?

28 Give an account of any story you have read in which the principal character is a criminal: try to assess the reasons why he (or she) has adopted this way of life.

29 Describe carefully how coincidence has played a major role in any novel or play you have read.

30 Sometimes in a novel or play one comes across a character who can be described as 'eccentric' or 'grotesque' in physical appearance or behaviour. If you have encountered such a type in your reading, show how his or her 'oddity' is significant in the story or its plot.

Suggested notes for an essay answer to question 1

(a) Obvious basis and intention of entire novel: a social, industrial and political issue, but concentrating on education – the prohibiting of development of 'feelings'.

(b) Education at school and home: opening schoolroom sequence; later fairground/circus detail; Stone Lodge and 'Never wonder'.

(c) Appeal of circus, and why: Louisa and Tom's 'delinquency' in peeping through fence: their separate reactions when discovered.

(d) Sissy Jupe – consequences of her father's abandonment – moved from one 'system' to another, and is unaffected.

(e) Tom and Louisa affected in different ways – Tom towards criminal activity (involving others), and Louisa's dangerous involvement with Harthouse – both victims of the 'system'.

(f) Scattered, isolated instances of Gradgrind's wavering between Fact and Fancy as story develops: culmination in awakening shock of Louisa's revelations.

(g) Mrs Gradgrind's eventual recognition of the world of the imagination.

(h) Bounderby and Bitzer unchanged throughout – effect of this upon others' lives.

(i) Conclusion: brief overview of the consequences, in general of the Fact and Fancy tensions, and Dickens's prophecies of their future resolution.

Brodie's Notes

TITLES IN THE SERIES

Edward Albee	Who's Afraid of Virginia Woolf?
Jane Austen	Emma
Jane Austen	Mansfield Park
Jane Austen	Pride and Prejudice
Samuel Beckett	Waiting for Godot
William Blake	Songs of Innocence and Experience
Robert Bolt	A Man for All Seasons
Charlotte Brontë	Jane Eyre
Emily Brontë	Wuthering Heights
Geoffrey Chaucer	The Franklin's Tale
Geoffrey Chaucer	The Knight's Tale
Geoffrey Chaucer	The Miller's Tale
Geoffrey Chaucer	The Nun's Priest's Tale
Geoffrey Chaucer	The Pardoner's Prologue and Tale
Geoffrey Chaucer	Prologue to the Canterbury Tales
Geoffrey Chaucer	The Wife of Bath's Tale
Wilkie Collins	Woman in White
Joseph Conrad	Heart of Darkness
Charles Dickens	Great Expectations
Charles Dickens	Hard Times
Charles Dickens	Oliver Twist
Charles Dickens	A Tale of Two Cities
Gerald Durrell	My Family and Other Animals
George Eliot	Silas Marner
T. S. Eliot	Selected Poems
Henry Fielding	Tom Jones
F. Scott Fitzgerald	The Great Gatsby and Tender is the Night
E. M. Forster	Howard's End
E. M. Forster	A Passage to India
John Fowles	The French Lieutenant's Woman
Anne Frank	The Diary of Anne Frank
Mrs Gaskell	North and South
William Golding	Lord of the Flies
Graham Greene	Brighton Rock
Graham Greene	The Power and the Glory
Graham Handley (ed)	The Metaphysical Poets: John Donne to Henry Vaughan
Thomas Hardy	Far From the Madding Crowd
Thomas Hardy	The Mayor of Casterbridge
Thomas Hardy	The Return of the Native
Thomas Hardy	Tess of the D'Urbervilles
L. P. Hartley	The Go-Between
Aldous Huxley	Brave New World
James Joyce	Portrait of the Artist as a Young Man
John Keats	Selected Poems and Letters of John Keats
Philip Larkin	Selected Poems of Philip Larkin

D. H. Lawrence	**The Rainbow**
D. H. Lawrence	**Sons and Lovers**
D. H. Lawrence	**Women in Love**
Harper Lee	**To Kill a Mockingbird**
Laurie Lee	**Cider with Rosie**
Christopher Marlowe	**Dr Faustus**
Arthur Miller	**The Crucible**
Arthur Miller	**Death of a Salesman**
John Milton	**Paradise Lost**
Robert C. O'Brien	**Z for Zachariah**
Sean O'Casey	**Juno and the Paycock**
George Orwell	**Animal Farm**
George Orwell	**1984**
J. B. Priestley	**An Inspector Calls**
J. D. Salinger	**The Catcher in the Rye**
William Shakespeare	**Antony and Cleopatra**
William Shakespeare	**As You Like It**
William Shakespeare	**Hamlet**
William Shakespeare	**Henry IV Part I**
William Shakespeare	**Julius Caesar**
William Shakespeare	**King Lear**
William Shakespeare	**Macbeth**
William Shakespeare	**Measure for Measure**
William Shakespeare	**The Merchant of Venice**
William Shakespeare	**A Midsummer Night's Dream**
William Shakespeare	**Much Ado about Nothing**
William Shakespeare	**Othello**
William Shakespeare	**Richard II**
William Shakespeare	**Romeo and Juliet**
William Shakespeare	**The Tempest**
William Shakespeare	**Twelfth Night**
George Bernard Shaw	**Pygmalion**
Alan Sillitoe	**Selected Fiction**
John Steinbeck	**Of Mice and Men and The Pearl**
Jonathan Swift	**Gulliver's Travels**
Dylan Thomas	**Under Milk Wood**
Alice Walker	**The Color Purple**
W. B. Yeats	**Selected Poetry**

ENGLISH COURSEWORK BOOKS

Terri Apter	**Women and Society**
Kevin Dowling	**Drama and Poetry**
Philip Gooden	**Conflict**
Philip Gooden	**Science Fiction**
Margaret K. Gray	**Modern Drama**
Graham Handley	**Modern Poetry**
Graham Handley	**Prose**
Graham Handley	**Childhood and Adolescence**
R. J. Sims	**The Short Story**